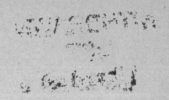

BUSINESS-CYCLE THEORY

ITS DEVELOPMENT
AND PRESENT STATUS

BY

ALVIN HARVEY HANSEN, Ph.D.

PROFESSOR OF ECONOMICS, UNIVERSITY OF MINNESOTA

GINN AND COMPANY

BOSTON · NEW YORK · CHICAGO · LONDON
ATLANTA · DALLAS · COLUMBUS · SAN FRANCISCO

𝕿𝖍𝖊 𝕬𝖙𝖍𝖊𝖓𝖆𝖚𝖒 𝕻𝖗𝖊𝖘𝖘

GINN AND COMPANY · PRO-
PRIETORS · BOSTON · U.S.A.

PREFACE

In my earlier monograph, *Cycles of Prosperity and Depression* (1921), I made a study of cyclical fluctuations in the United States, Great Britain, and Germany for the period 1902–1908. After making a classification of various business-cycle theories, I offered certain conclusions, derived from the statistical portions of my study, which supported the monetary theory of the business cycle. Since then I have come to take a less dogmatic position. In the present work I have endeavored to synthesize the views of those writers who have made, as I see it, important contributions to the theory of the business cycle.

While I have drawn upon numerous writers, I have not been concerned to give a detailed analysis of the work of each author; rather, I have sought to show the development and significance of the various *theories* and their relation to each other.

I have endeavored to present a balanced and unified view of the complex causes of the business-cycle phenomenon. The conclusion drawn from the consideration of these causes is that there is a surprisingly large measure of agreement among the leading business-cycle theorists, despite the apparent irreconcilable antagonism which is often met. Yet, I have tried not to fall into the error of superficially accepting all theories as partly true, if in fact they are mutually exclusive. It has been my purpose, not merely to give the student or general reader a survey of business-cycle theories, but to help him to cut a path through the tangled mass of apparently contradictory explanations of the business cycle.

Many economists seem to believe that it is necessary to take a completely agnostic position with respect to the causes of the business cycle. As a result of my study, it does not seem to me that business-cycle theory is in quite this hopeless condition. It seems to me that the foundation principles for a substantial theory of the business cycle have been developed during the last quarter century or so, particularly by Tougan-Baranowsky and Spiethoff; Carver, Aftalion, Bickerdike, and Clark; Wicksell, Fisher, and Hawtrey; Veblen and Mitchell. Important work, largely of a synthesizing nature, has also been done by Robertson, Cassel, and Pigou. Many others have contributed, but the groupings of names above indicate the main strands of thought which I have tried to weave into a unified synthesis.

The first seven chapters of this monograph, somewhat differently arranged but in substantially the form in which they here appear, were submitted under the title *Profits: a Critical Analysis in the Light of Business Cycle Theories* as an essay in the Pollak Prize Contest, in which it was given honorable mention. The judges were Owen D. Young of the General Electric Company, Allyn A. Young of Harvard University, and Wesley

C. Mitchell of Columbia University. The fact that
these chapters were submitted in this contest explains
the considerable space devoted to the theory of Foster
and Catchings. In the consideration of these writers,
however, the general literature of the business cycle is
drawn upon so heavily that the inclusion of this material is felt to be thoroughly justified in a general work
on business-cycle theory.

I am indebted to my colleagues Professor F. B. Garver
and Professor Walter R. Myers, of the University of
Minnesota, and to Dr. Robert M. Weidenhammer,
formerly a German-American Fellow in the University
of Minnesota, for reading the entire manuscript and
offering helpful suggestions. It is of course understood
that none of the gentlemen mentioned are responsible
for any of the shortcomings that may appear in the work.

My thanks are also due my brother-in-law, Dr. C. E.
Peters, for assistance with the German and for reading
the entire proof. Finally, I am indebted to my wife for
her interest in the progress of the work and her help
with the reading of the proof.

I desire to take this occasion to express my apprecia-
tion of Dr. Willford I. King, formerly of the University
of Wisconsin and now of the staff of the National
Bureau of Economic Research, who first stimulated my
interest in the study of the business cycle.

ALVIN H. HANSEN

MINNEAPOLIS, MINNESOTA

CONTENTS

BUSINESS–CYCLE THEORY

CHAPTER I

A CLASSIFICATION OF BUSINESS–CYCLE THEORIES

In the opinion of the present writer it is quite possible to make a classification of business-cycle *theories*, but dangerous, on the whole, to classify *theorists*. A rigid classification of writers, in which each writer is placed in a single category, implies that every writer is monistic or unilateral in his views. As a matter of fact few writers give a single, monistic explanation of the business cycle. The business cycle is such a complex phenomenon that it may almost be accepted a priori that a unilateral explanation is false or at least partial and incomplete. And in point of fact this is well recognized by most of the writers on the subject. The theories, in many cases, are not mutually exclusive, and there is therefore no inherent reason why one and the same writer may not appear as an exponent of several complementary and mutually supporting theories. Accordingly I have not hesitated to place the same name under two or more heads in the classifica-

1

tion that follows. Any one grouping, considered without relation to the rest, is therefore misleading.

The writer is fully aware, even though this precaution against rigidity is taken, that classifications are dangerous. There are marked differences, often, between the writers placed in the same categories — differences that can only be fully sensed by reading the authors themselves. In point of fact we are not much concerned with whether or not a certain writer belongs to this or that group. We are only concerned with the development of the theory under discussion; and at times, in developing a certain theory, writers who could scarcely be classified in the category in question have been drawn upon merely because they have said something which helps toward an understanding of that theory.

It is a well-accepted and commonplace fact that the business cycle is a modern phenomenon — a product of the modern economic order with its technical conditions and legal institutions. The business cycle can obviously not be understood without taking account of the structure, organization, functions, and processes of the existing economic society. The business cycle is firmly rooted in the technological processes of production, in the legal-economic institutions by means of which goods are exchanged and distributed to the various coöperating classes, and in the responses of human beings to these man-made, institutional stimuli, as well as to those offered by the external, material world itself.

There are three broad types of business-cycle theories with subgroups and classes. In the first place, there are those who hold that the business cycle is a function of the capitalistic economy. This group in turn comprises two main schools. There are, first, those who view the capitalistic economy from the standpoint of distribution, who believe that the legal-economic institutions are controlling, and that maladjustments in the distribution of income are the moving forces which throw production and consumption out of equilibrium and create fluctuations of output. The capitalistic economy operating under existing legal-economic institutions gives rise to gross inequality in the distribution of income. There follows, from this concentration of income, a tendency to accumulate vast fortunes which are invested in instruments of production. At this point this group of theorists are forced to recognize the technological character of the capitalistic economy — the fact that the modern machine method of production is a roundabout, time-consuming process. Consumers' goods are made indirectly by first making producers' goods — instruments of production. There arises, therefore, the problem of the proper relation between consumption and production, between spending and saving. But this group of theorists do not find that the maladjustment of consumption and production springs from the technological character of the capitalistic method of production; they find it rather in the legal-economic institutions of the existing capitalistic order, by means of which the product is distributed in a certain manner. It is in the distributive process that underconsumption and over-saving emerge. In their view, therefore, the evil of fluctuations in output and income can be remedied by changing the legal-economic institutions but leaving intact the technological basis (the roundabout, machine method of production) of the capitalistic economy. Among the theorists belonging to this group are Lauderdale, Malthus, Sismondi, Marx, John A. Hobson, and Bouniatian.

The second school of theorists, who also hold that the business cycle is a function of the capitalistic economy, center their attention on the technological character of the modern economic order. They are therefore less optimistic that the business cycle can be eliminated. They hold that it is, in large part at any rate, an inevitable consequence of the nature of the modern productive process, particularly so long as that process is subject to the dynamic influences of inventions, new discoveries, new resources, improved methods, increasing capital accumulation, and increasing population. The business cycle is held to be a function of economic progress in a society using a capitalistic, or roundabout, method of production. From this point of view the business cycle is firmly rooted in the technological basis of modern society.

It is the roundabout, time-consuming process of the capitalistic economy that this group of theorists calls attention to. With them the cycle consists of fluctuations in the output of instrumental goods — machines, factories, railroads, ships, and other equipment which it requires much time to produce, and which in turn function (in the process of making consumers' goods) over a long period of time. Out of the time element, the roundabout method of production characteristic of the capitalistic economy, and the uncertainties, contingencies, and errors of judgment consequent thereto, arise maladjustments in the proportion of the total national income directed toward the purchase of producers' goods compared with the purchase of consumers' goods; maladjustments in the quantity of instruments produced and the quantity of savings available for their purchase and operation; maladjustments between the quantity of instruments produced and the quantity of complementary factors — raw materials and labor — available to operate them; maladjustments growing out of the fact that in the modern order consumers' goods are produced by the indirect process of first producing capital goods.

This group of theories comprises, in turn, two subclasses: (1) those who find that inventions, discoveries, and technical innovations are the impelling forces which disrupt the economic equilibrium and (2) those who find the impelling forces in changes in consumer demand. To the former belong, as we shall see, Marx, Tougan-Baranowsky, Spiethoff, Schumpeter, Cassel, Robertson, Adams, and others (see Chapter IV below);

to the latter belong, among others, Aftalion, Pigou, Carver, J. M. Clark, and Bickerdike.

Our second main division comprises the theories which hold that the business cycle is a function of the competitive exchange economy. The market in such an economy is distant both in time and space; the more distant it is, the more complex are the division of labor and the specialization of industry. It is an uncertain, contingent market, fraught with speculation and risks. In such an economy, business men produce, borrow money, employ labor, buy raw material and equipment on the basis of expectancies of future results. Miscalculations occur; errors of judgment that are likely to become cumulative are bound to arise. And these are all the more pronounced in view of the fact that in the modern individualistic exchange economy competition rules to a large extent. It follows that each firm acts without knowledge of what others in the same trade are doing. Moreover, the extreme division of labor and specialization involved in the modern exchange economy makes each group of producers dependent for a market on the group next in the chain of production. There results a high interdependence between producers, so that any situation affecting one group has a cumulative effect on other groups. Among the economists that belong to this group may be mentioned Beveridge, Marshall, Pigou, Taussig, Mitchell, Lescure, Allyn Young, Frank, King, and Lavington.

Finally, there is the theory that the business cycle is a function of the money economy. With this group the fact that the technological processes of production, the legal-economic institutions that govern distribution, and the individual exchange economy and market processes function through the money and credit mechanism is of primary importance; and it is in the functioning of this mechanism that we must seek for light with respect to the phenomena of cyclical fluctuations. In the modern economy, demand and supply run in terms of money units of measurement. Price fluctuations are a result not of the processes of production and consumption per se, but of the offers of money and credit against goods and services. Thus an explanation of the business cycle must be sought in price fluctuations; in the relations of the rate of profit, the rate of discount, bank reserves, cash balances of producers and consumers, loans and bank credit; in the lag of costs behind selling prices; in profit margins; and in the ratio of current income to capitalization. Among writers belonging to this group we may mention Juglar, Sidgwick, Giffen, Marshall, Wicksell, Fisher, Hawtrey, Allyn Young, Veblen, Lescure, Mitchell, Pigou, Röpke, and Hahn.

Some writers are unilateral, others eclectic in their views. Of the former group, most writers take the view that while the business cycle is fundamentally conditioned or caused by a single characteristic feature of the

economic system, yet other characteristic institutions
serve as media through which the initial impulse is
transmitted, or else reënforce and so intensify the
initial movement. Many of the writers who belong to
the Capitalistic Production and Exchange Economy
schools take this view of the influence of the money
economy on the business cycle. They refuse to admit
that the causes of the business cycle can be found in
the money economy, but they are quite willing to admit
that the money economy is either a conditioning factor[1]
or else a reënforcing factor intensifying movements
started by other forces. These writers believe that the
business cycle is not caused by "forces" inherent in
the money economy, but that its *form* and *intensity* are
profoundly affected by the money institutions through
which the modern economic order works. Few, if any,
writers are *completely* unilateral in their views; few
refuse to admit that any other factor (except the one
adhered to) has any consequence so far as the business
cycle is concerned.

Many writers are eclectic or pluralistic in their views.
They hold that causal factors must be sought in several
characteristics of the modern order. They refuse to
admit that certain characteristics are alone controlling,
while others are merely supplementary, reënforcing,
or modifying in their influence. The causal forces are

[1]Cf. Arthur Spiethoff, "Krisen," *Handwörterbuch der Staatswissen-schaften* (1925), VI, pp. 72–74, 81–82.

conceived of as pluralistic or at least dualistic rather than monistic.

The line between the unilateral thinkers and the pluralistic thinkers can be drawn by asking the question Would the business cycle disappear if the characteristic in question were not present? Those who believe that the business cycle would disappear were the money economy, for example, eliminated are clearly unilateral or monistic in their views. Examples of relatively unilateral thinkers belonging to the various schools are Hobson of the Capitalistic Distribution school, Spiethoff of the first subgroup of the Capitalistic Production school, Aftalion of the second subgroup of this school, Beveridge of the Exchange Economy school, and Hawtrey of the Money Economy school.

Examples of dualistic and pluralistic thinkers are Lescure, who belongs to the Exchange Economy and Money Economy schools; Cassel, who belongs to the Capitalistic Production and Money Economy schools; J. M. Clark, who belongs to the Capitalistic Production and Exchange Economy schools; Marx, who belongs to the Capitalistic Distribution and Capitalistic Production schools; and finally Wesley Mitchell, Taussig, Allyn Young, and Pigou, who are broadly eclectic, giving weight to factors emphasized by the Capitalistic Production, Exchange Economy, and Money Economy schools. Many other writers could be mentioned, but these will serve as illustrations.

These various schools are discussed in the next five chapters. The following is a classification of the groups briefly described above.[1]

I. The Capitalistic Economy schools
   A. The capitalistic system of distribution as cause of the business cycle
   B. The capitalistic process of production as cause of the business cycle
      1. Inventions, discoveries, and innovations as impelling factors disturbing the economic equilibrium
      2. Fluctuations in consumers' demand as impelling factor disturbing the economic equilibrium
II. The Exchange Economy school
III. The Money Economy schools
   A. The interrelations of the rate of interest, the prospective rate of profit, and the price level
   B. The interrelations of costs and prices, profit margins, and capitalization

[1] Our classification does not include as a special group the crop-cycle theories of Jevons and Moore. Their theory is, however, taken account of in Chapter IV along with those theories which find the cause of cyclical fluctuations in the material basis of our modern economic order. It is of course clear that fluctuations in the bounty of nature do not in and of themselves produce business cycles. Only in so far as the impact of these fluctuations in nature's generosity is brought to bear upon the complex mechanism of the modern capitalistic order with its exchange and money institutions do they generate or modify, as the case may be, industrial or business fluctuations. Yet the present writer does not deny that there may be justification for a separate classification of this theory; he has, however, not found it useful to make such a classification.

CHAPTER II

THE CAPITALISTIC SYSTEM OF DISTRIBUTION AS CAUSE OF THE BUSINESS CYCLE

Lord Lauderdale,[1] the first representative of the Capitalistic Distribution school, speaking of a nation's prosperity, remarked that "the extent to which the exertions of its industry, and even its population, can be pushed, depends upon the distribution of its wealth."[2] And this because of the effect of wealth distribution upon consumption and accumulation of capital. It is "at once evident that, as the means of consuming must, at all times, limit the quantity of labor that can be employed in preparing things for consumption, so it must limit the amount of capital that can be used in coöperating with the hands of man, for the purpose of performing labor, and that, in proportion as forced parsimony abstracts from the funds that would be allotted to acquire consumable commodities, the demand for labor, whether performed by the hand of man or by capital, must be diminished."[3] A right proportion must be maintained between spending and saving.

[1] *An Inquiry into the Nature and Origin of Public Wealth* (1804; 2d ed., 1819).
[2] Op. cit. (2d ed.) p. 364.
[3] Ibid. pp. 262–263.

11

Malthus[1] was the next great English economist[2] to take up the cudgels against the overaccumulation of capital. Malthus was quite willing to admit that capital was quite deficient compared with the population, but he would not admit that it was deficient (he was writing during the post-Napoleonic depression) compared with "the demand for it, and the demand for the commodities procured by it."[3] Production, though decidedly deficient compared with the population, "is redundant, compared with the effectual demand for it and the revenue which is to purchase it."[4] The "low profits of stock" and the difficulty of finding employment for it, Malthus considered unequivocal proof that the immediate want of the country was not capital. The "stagnation which has been so generally felt and complained of since the war, appears to me inexplicable

[1] T. R. Malthus, *Principles of Political Economy* (1820).

[2] S. de Sismondi (*Nouveaux principes* (1819)) was the French representative of the overproduction theory. Sismondi argued that "last year's revenue pays for the production of this." If the production of this year exceeds the revenue of last year, a portion of the produce will remain unsold. See C. Gide and C. Rist, *History of Economic Doctrines* (D. C. Heath & Co.), pp. 176–177. See also M. Bouniatian's criticism of Sismondi in his article "Ma Théorie des crises," *Revue d'économie politique* (1924), p. 668. Sismondi's analysis reminds one of W. T. Foster and Waddill Catchings's statement that "time is the essence of the problem." He finally admitted the identity of production and consumption under conditions of perfect circulation of goods. But this "involves making an abstraction of time and place, and of all those obstacles which might arrest this circulation" (Gide and Rist, *History of Economic Doctrines*, p. 177).

[3] Malthus, op. cit. p. 379.

[4] Ibid. p. 382.

upon the principles of those who think that the power
of production is the only element of wealth and who
consequently infer that if the powers of production be
increased, wealth will certainly increase in proportion." [1]
The trouble is rather a "great diminution of the whole
amount of consumption and demand." [2] This contraction of demand was caused by the cessation of war expenditures, the reduction of taxes, and the consequent
increase in saving. "We should constantly bear in mind
that the tendency to expenditure in individuals has
most formidable antagonists in the love of indolence,
and in the desire of saving, in order to better their condition and provide for a family; and that all theories
founded upon the assumption, that mankind always
produce and consume as much as they have the power
to produce and consume, are founded upon a want of
knowledge of the human character, and of the motives
by which it is usually influenced." [3]

But now how increase the effective demand for consumables? Malthus believed that a more equal distribution of wealth would help. Despite certain evils
attendant upon the increase in the public debt, he
wondered whether these were not "more than counter-

---

[1] Ibid. p. 385. See also page 390, as follows: "If at the very time
that the supply of commodities to revenue is already too great, we go
on saving from our revenue to add still further to our capital, all general
principles concur in showing that we must of necessity be aggravating
instead of alleviating our distresses."

[2] Ibid. p. 386.

[3] Ibid. p. 389.

balanced by the distribution of property and income in the middle class of society, which it must necessarily create."[1] A more equal distribution of land would be desirable from the standpoint of the problem in hand, but Malthus opposed this on broad grounds of social policy.[2] Instead he favored the increased maintenance by landlords of "unproductive" laborers. "It is also important to know that, in our endeavor to assist the working classes in a period like the present, it is desirable to employ them in unproductive labors, or at least in labor, the results of which do not come for sale into the market, such as roads and public works."[3]

Karl Marx[4] held that the conditions of direct exploitation of labor and those of the realization of surplus value (profit) are not identical. "The first are only limited by the productive power of society, the last by the proportional relations of the various lines of production and by the consuming power of society."[5] The consuming power is restricted by the "tendency to accumulate, the greed for an expansion of capital and a

---

[1] Malthus, p. 392. Compare with the following by Foster and Catchings: "If, for example, there were only five million stockholders, a larger part of the dividends will be saved, and a smaller proportion spent, than would be the case if there were ten million owners" (*Profits*, p. 357).

[2] Ibid. pp. 391–392.

[3] Ibid. p. 395. Cf. Foster and Catchings (see Chapter III of this book).

[4] Karl Marx and F. Engels, *Communist Manifesto* (1848); *Capital* (1894), Vol. III.

[5] *Capital*, Vol. III, chap. xv.

production of surplus-value on an enlarged scale. . . .
But to the extent that the productive power develops,
it finds itself at variance with the narrow basis on which
the conditions of consumption rest." [1] "Finally, if it is
said that the capitalists would only have to exchange
and consume the commodities among themselves, then
the nature of the capitalist mode of production is
forgotten; it is forgotten, that the question is merely
one of expanding the value of the capital, not of consuming it." [2]

John A. Hobson [3] has restated the argument of his
predecessors, but has contributed little, if any, to their
work. The full, regular employment of the factors of
production demands the maintenance of a proper proportion between the production of consumable commodities and that of capital goods. There exists at any
given time an economically sound ratio between spending and saving. Under fairly equal distribution of income a right adjustment between spending and saving
might be expected to be maintained. But the existing

[1] Ibid.

[2] Ibid. Note also Marx's statement that there can be a lack of demand for the very commodities which the mass of the people want "because in this specific capitalist interrelation the surplus-product assumes
a form in which its owner cannot offer it for consumption, unless it first
reconverts itself into capital for him." Compare this with Foster and
Catchings's statement that money used twice in the production of goods
before it is used in the consumption of goods creates a deficiency of
consumer demand.

[3] John A. Hobson, *The Industrial System* (Charles Scribner's Sons,
1909); *The Economics of Unemployment* (George Allen & Unwin,
Limited, 1922).

distribution of income tends to work a rate of saving that is excessive. This arises from the circumstance that the surplus incomes of the rich are excessive even for purposes of luxurious and wasteful consumption, and hence they accumulate automatically in the form of an excessive supply of capital.[1] The remedy lies in strengthening the consuming powers of the community, so that effective demand for consumable goods may keep full pace with increased productivity. And consumption, he contends, may be strengthened by a better distribution of the product of industry. In this way an "economically right proportion between expenditure in withdrawing commodities from the retail shops for consumption, and expenditure in maintaining and enlarging the plant and industries functioning in each stage of production" can be maintained.[2]

M. Bouniatian [3] speaks of an "excessive tendency to accumulation," the "excessive desire to save." It is this tendency which pushes capital formation beyond the limits compatible with the effective social consumption. He admits that there can be no excess of production over purchasing power, but contends that it is the desire to use the power of purchasing for productive

[1] Hobson is not, of course, opposed to the accumulation of capital per se. His point is that if a smaller *proportion* of the national income were saved, production would be steadier, the total national income would be greater, and so the *absolute volume* of capital accumulation might well be greater than now.

[2] Cf. Foster and Catchings (see Chapter III of this book).

[3] "Ma Théorie des crises," *Revue d'économie politique* (1924).

ends in a proportion which is not compatible with the social consumption "which leads to the state of chronic overcapitalization."[1]

While overaccumulation is a grave evil, it does not, in Bouniatian's view, condemn the existing order. For even though the tendency to excessive accumulation gives rise to certain perturbations of the economic life, it assures at the same time, and in an automatic way, the rapid augmentation of capital and the elevation of standards for all classes. It is a great factor of economic progress which can be moderated and regulated.[2]

A position opposite to that of Lauderdale, Malthus, and Sismondi was taken by J. B. Say,[3] D. Ricardo,[4] James Mill,[5] and J. S. Mill.[6] These writers held that production can never be too rapid for demand, since demand depends on purchasing power, which in turn depends on the nation's aggregate production. General overproduction is impossible. Goods exchange against

[1] Op. cit., pp. 668–669. Bouniatian gives Lauderdale the credit for "signalling the danger of an excess of saving," but holds that it was Malthus who attributes the periodic overproduction to the excessive tendency to accumulate, which tendency is facilitated by the inequality of the distribution of wealth (p. 669).

[2] Ibid. p. 673.

[3] *Le Traité d'économie politique* (1803). Cf. Gide and Rist, *History of Economic Doctrines*, pp. 115–117.

[4] *Principles of Political Economy and Taxation* (1817). Cf. Gonner's edition, pp. 272–277.

[5] *Elements of Political Economy* (1821). Cf. 3d ed., pp. 228–245.

[6] *Principles of Political Economy* (1848). Cf. Ashley's edition, pp. 66–81, 556–563, 725–745.

goods. If the exchange value of one grade of goods is
too low, it follows that the exchange value of other goods
is too high. As a result, less of the former will be produced and more of the latter. There can be misdirected
production, but no general overproduction. No matter
how great the increase of capital or of productive efficiency, a market can always be found, for goods exchange against goods.

Suppose, says J. S. Mill, that capitalists and landlords decide, or are forced by law or opinion, to live no
better than workmen. They accordingly save all their
surplus income. "Unproductive expenditure," says
Mill, "is now reduced to its lowest limit, and, it is
asked, how is the increased capital to find employment?
Who is to buy the goods which it will produce? There
are no longer customers even for those which were produced before." But, Mill contends, this is only seeing
one half of the matter. The capitalists and landlords,
it is true, will no longer demand luxuries. But by in-
vesting their income they merely transfer their purchasing power from themselves to the laborers who
are employed to make the capital goods.[1]

An increased accumulation of capital involves first

[1] J. S. Mill, op. cit., pp. 67–68. This is similar to Foster and Catchings's
Cases V and VI (see Chapter III). While the capital goods are being
created the production-consumption equation is not disturbed. Foster
and Catchings, however, follow the matter out further and show that
when the capital goods are finally completed and begin to turn out
consumers' goods, the flow of goods into the retail markets will exceed
the flow of money into the hands of consumers, and so prices will fall.

a change in the proportion of the capital factor compared with the other factors of production, and eventually an increased output of finished goods. The first results in a fall in the income on capital (interest) and a rise in wages and economic rent;[1] the second involves a fall in prices unless counteracted by an increase in money incomes. Neither of these consequences implies that production has outrun consumption. In this Say, Ricardo, and Mill were right. But does it follow that neither of these consequences has any relation to the phenomena of business depressions?

Lauderdale and Malthus agreed with their opponents that an increase in the supply of capital tends to lower the rate of profit. Lauderdale said that "there must be, at all times, a point determined by the existing state of knowledge in the art of supplanting and performing labor with capital, beyond which capital cannot profitably be increased, and beyond which it will not naturally increase; because the quantity, when it exceeds that point, must increase in proportion to the demand for it, and its value, like that of all other commodities, must of consequence diminish in such a manner as effectively to check its augmentation."[2] Malthus remarked that if a "society were greatly and generally to slacken their consumption, and add to

---

[1] A fall in the interest rate means that a larger proportion of the national income is diverted from capitalists to laborers. Obviously it does not imply that production has outrun consumption.

[2] Lauderdale, op. cit., p. 225.

their capitals, there cannot be the least doubt . . . that
the profits of capitalists would soon be reduced to
nothing."[1] These statements are quite in line with
J. S. Mill, who argued that the net effect of oversaving
would be a fall in the rate of profit. "What would really
be not merely difficult, but impossible, would be to employ this capital without submitting to a rapid reduction of the rate of profit."[2] Note also the following
from James Mill:

The doctrine of Mr. Malthus, on the subject of the glut,
seems, at last, to amount to this: that if saving were to
go on at a certain rate, capital would increase faster than
population; and that if capital did so increase, wages
would become very high, and profits would sustain a
corresponding depression. But this, if it were all allowed,
does not prove the existence of a glut; it only proves
another thing, namely, that there would be high wages and
low profits. Whether such an increase of capital, scarcely
coming within the range even of a rational supposition,
would be a good thing or an evil thing, it would infallibly
produce its own remedy, as the power of capital to increase
is diminished with the diminution of profits.[3]

Lauderdale and Malthus agreed with their opponents that a fall in the rate of profit would automatically tend to check oversaving. What they really meant
to say was that you cannot usher in prosperity by

[1] Malthus, op. cit., p. 384.
[2] J. S. Mill, op. cit., p. 732.
[3] James Mill, op. cit., p. 242.

artificially stimulating capital accumulation during the
period of depression. Lauderdale argued against a proposal to raise by governmental action "fifteen millions
for the purpose of accumulation" by "forcibly convert-
ing fifteen millions of revenue into capital." He opposed
a "forced increase of capital."[1] Malthus was of the
opinion that "if it were true that, in order to employ
all that are out of work, and to create at the same time
a sufficient market for what they produce, it is only
necessary that a little more should be saved from the
revenue and added to the capital of the country, I am
fully persuaded that this species of charity will not
want contributors, and that the change would soon be
wrought in the condition of the laboring classes."[2] In
this they were quite right. Their opponents thought
that "industry is limited by capital." Any measure,
whether reduced taxes or lower wages, which would increase the income of capitalists and so stimulate saving
would, they thought, work to dissipate depression.
Mill and Ricardo understood no better than Lauderdale
and Malthus the disrupting forces which had disturbed the economic equilibrium and which made it
impossible for industry to operate at capacity.

Neither of the two opposing schools understood the
significance of the other possible result of increased
capital accumulation; namely, the increased output
of finished goods and the consequent fall in prices.

[1] Lauderdale, op. cit., pp. 243–244, 248, 260.
[2] Malthus, op. cit., p. 391.

J. S. Mill admitted this possibility, but he thought it of no consequence. He failed to take account of the price maladjustments that accompany price declines.

In a crisis there is "really an excess of all commodities above the money demand: in other words, there is an undersupply of money."[1] There may thus be an "extreme depression of prices, from what may be indiscriminately called a glut of commodities or a dearth of money." But what of it? "If values remained the same what becomes of prices is immaterial, since the remuneration of producers does not depend on how much money, but on how much of consumable articles, they obtain for their goods." That the decline of prices is, however, contrary to Mill's view, of utmost importance in the phenomenon of the business cycle is now well established, particularly through the researches of Mitchell, Veblen, Lescure, Fisher, and Hawtrey. This aspect of the matter will, however, receive treatment in a later chapter.

John A. Hobson, in his criticism of the classicals with respect to this point, fails to see the matter clearly. He denies that a fall in prices is an equilibrating factor, tending to increase consumption, to restore the balance between the demand for and the supply of goods.[2] In this he is quite right; but he fails to see that when the classicals and neoclassicals speak of a fall in price as an equilibrating factor, they are thinking of an economic

[1] J. S. Mill, op. cit., p. 561.
[2] *Economics of Unemployment*, pp. 53–57.

force of the static supply-and-demand variety.[1] In the dynamics of the business cycle the fall in prices is a tremendously powerful disrupting factor. This is in line with Hobson's criticism. But if he had followed this point out into all its ramifications he would not have been able to discount the influence of monetary factors in the business cycle, but would have been forced into a thoroughgoing analysis of the reasons why prices fall in the depression, and also why falling prices produce such disastrous effects upon business. This would have led him into an analysis of the lag of costs behind selling prices, the margin of profits, current income in relation to capitalization, prime and supplementary costs, and the maladjustments that force a curtailment of production. Holding fast to his consumption-and-production base, he was unable to follow out the lead here given to its logical conclusions.

Two meanings may be properly attached to the term "limited market." In the first place, there may be a limited market in the sense that there is not a sufficient quantity of money offered by buyers to take the goods off the market at the existing level of prices. Say's law of markets failed to take into account the money econ-

[1] Note the following significant statement from J. M. Clark: "The distinguishing characteristic of economic forces of the supply and demand variety ... is that they are self-limiting; the more they prevail the weaker they become, and the stronger grows the resistance. The business cycle forces are, however, cumulative and self-reinforcing." — *Economics of Overhead Cost*, p. 388.   The University of Chicago Press

omy.[1] As is pointed out by F. M. Taylor, the "law of markets" holds good only in the long run. And this is true for the reason that except "under the most primitive conditions, every exchange of product for product is broken into two parts (1) exchanging one's own product for money or bank credits and (2) exchanging the money or bank credits thus obtained for the product of the other man. Obviously, an interval of time can be put between these two operations; and as a matter of fact, such an interval, short or long, almost always intervenes. It follows . . . that it is possible for us to postpone for a long period, even indefinitely, the second part of the operation, thus cutting down for the time being the general demand for goods, though we have not cut down the amount of production. On the other hand, it is possible that, by getting possession of the medium of exchange, money or bank credits, in ways other than by exchanging our goods for that medium of exchange, we should perform the second half of the exchange operation before having performed the first half. In this way demand may be increased enormously, though production has not been increased at all. . . . But the case is very different if . . . buyers generally are suspending the second half of the exchange operation. Such a procedure means a general decline in demand, hence of necessity a general slackening of productivity all along the line. A situation like this

---

[1] Cf. Alfred Marshall, *Principles of Economics* (7th ed.), pp. 710–711. Macmillan & Company, Limited.

is characteristic of the depression which follows a business crisis. If now, under such a condition of things the public authorities step in and undertake a large program of road-building or building construction or harbor improvements, this will really mean a considerable increase in total demand and so an increase in general prosperity." [1] Similarly, Hawtrey points out that with respect to the government policy of execution of public works in periods of depression the additional public expenditure must be met, if it is to improve employment, not out of increased taxation but by the creation of greater purchasing power through increased borrowing at the bank. [2]

The term "limited market" may also be used to indicate that the marginal utility of the goods offered in exchange does not equal the marginal disutility or sacrifice involved in production. This gets at the problem from the angle of the producer. Producers cannot find employment that will yield them sufficient returns to induce them to undertake the effort. As D. H. Robertson has remarked, there may be general overproduction in terms of sacrifice and utility. The point may be reached where the "effort demand for commodities in general becomes inelastic." [3]

It is clear, however, that this phase of the matter has

[1] F. M. Taylor, *Principles of Economics*, pp. 202–203. The Ronald Press Company, 1921.

[2] *Economic Journal*, March, 1926, p. 98.

[3] D. H. Robertson, *A Study of Industrial Fluctuations*, p. 200. P. S. King and Son, Limited.

to do with the total national product and income from
a long-run standpoint. It accounts for a considerable
amount of continuous unemployment. It accounts in
part for the limited purchasing power and limited
market found in many backward unprogressive countries, whose people lack ambition and energy. But it is
difficult to see that this sort of limited market has anything to do with the cyclical fluctuations of business.
These fluctuations are the product of human behavior
motivated not by considerations of disutility or sacrifice,
but by pecuniary considerations of the sort that face
the entrepreneur. Mr. D. H. Robertson's recent attempt [1] to show that entrepreneurs have a high elasticity of demand in terms of effort is not very convincing.
As Hawtrey points out,[2] the decision of the employer
as to the output of his business is in no way dependent
upon his own personal exertions; in fact, a restricted
output may easily give him more trouble than capacity
production.

[1] D. H. Robertson, *Banking Policy and the Price Level*, p. 20. P. S.
King and Son, Limited.
  [2] *Economic Journal*, September, 1926, p. 418.

CHAPTER III

THE THEORY OF FOSTER AND CATCHINGS IN COMPARISON WITH THE CAPITALISTIC-DISTRIBUTION THEORIES

It is not the purpose of this chapter to give a summary of the whole contents of *Profits*. We shall proceed at once to an analysis of the main argument. In order to do so it will be necessary to make a thorough statement of the illustrative cases by which the authors of *Profits* have developed their central thesis.[1] In doing so we shall not simply paraphrase the authors' words. We shall elaborate the cases in our own way and at the same time adhere strictly to the fundamental position taken in *Profits*. Having elaborated their illustrative cases, we shall then reduce their argument to its lowest terms and show precisely what points are involved. We shall then be in a position to examine in later chapters the theory of Foster and Catchings in relation to other business-cycle theories. This will prepare the way for a final evaluation of their thesis.

Let us consider in detail the argument presented in *Profits*. Concrete cases are given showing how the

[1] William T. Foster and Waddill Catchings, *Profits*, Part V. Houghton Mifflin Company.

circuit flow of money from consumer back to consumer is affected by certain business practices in the modern order. To begin with, certain fundamental assumptions are made: (1) Complete integration of industry, vertical and horizontal, in a single corporation. (2) This integrated corporation is the source of all consumers' income, and all the money disbursed by the corporation is paid in the form of wages or dividends. (3) The price level remains unchanged. (4) The volume of circulating media remains unchanged. (5) The velocity of money remains unchanged. (6) There are no taxes or governmental expenditures. (7) The wages are paid as goods are produced, and goods are sold and dividends paid in the succeeding unit of time. (8) All wages and dividends are spent for goods in the unit of time in which they are received. These assumptions are merely to make the exposition easier, and in the course of the argument many of these assumptions are withdrawn so as to conform more nearly with the facts of the actual world.

In Case I it is assumed that all the goods produced are consumers' goods, and that the money received from the sale of the goods is all distributed in wages. We may diagram the situation as follows:

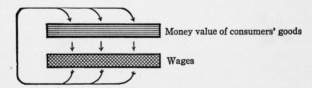

Money value of consumers' goods

Wages

In this diagram the barred area represents the money value of consumers' goods, and the crisscrossed area the money wages received. Labor is represented as the sole agent of production, and the full value of its product flows to it in the form of wages. The wages, in turn, are spent on the consumers' goods that labor has produced. Thus we have an equilibrium of supply and demand and no tendency in the direction of a change in prices.

In Case II a new situation is introduced. The money received from the sale of the goods is distributed in part to labor in the form of wages, and in part to capitalists in the form of dividends. The value of the products thus flows to two groups of sharers. Presumably the payment made in the form of dividends is not a mere gift, but is paid as a reward for a function performed in the process of production. The function performed by the dividend receivers is in part, let us say, that of risk taking, in part that of furnishing capital, or, in the more technical language of the economists, of "waiting" or saving. We may represent the process of production as having now become indirect or roundabout. Labor is applied directly in the production of machines, tools, and capital equipment, which in turn are worn out in the process of making consumers' goods. But labor could not engage in the roundabout method of production unless it was financed in the undertaking; unless capitalists were ready to make the necessary "advances"; or, to put it another way, unless someone was willing to sink present purchasing power in these production goods, which will only be able to yield consumers' goods gradually and piecemeal and over a considerable period of time. That is to say, a machine is worth something only because you can get consumers' goods out of it. But you cannot get the goods out of it all at once. You have to wear it out in the process of production, and bit by bit the consumers' goods emerge. In the meantime purchasing power is stored away in the machine and is not available for consumption. The roundabout or machine process of production cannot be engaged in unless someone is willing and able to finance it; that is to say, unless someone is willing and able to save, to "wait." "Waiting" is thus as necessary to the roundabout method of production as is labor itself.

Labor and waiting are thus combined in a joint venture of production. The joint functions of labor and waiting, however, do not produce consumers' goods directly: the first and immediate product is capital goods, and these capital goods, in turn, produce consumers' goods. Let us say that the machinery automatically turns out consumers' goods (without the aid of labor to tend it), and that all labor is devoted exclusively to the production of capital goods. But the capital goods do not, let us say, yield their full measure of consumers' goods in a year: it takes, it may be, several years for them to wear out and yield their full quota of consumers' goods. Let us say that three annual increments of consumers' goods emerge before each batch of capital

goods is worn out; a third of the potential consumers'
goods which the instrumental goods are capable of
yielding is given off each year. If, now, labor replaces
one third of the existing equipment each year, the total
quantity of capital goods will remain intact. While
labor is replacing the capital worn out, indirectly it may
be said to produce the batch of consumers' goods that
the machines yield each year. We may picture the
capital goods as three potential bundles of consumers'
goods, one of which is given off each year, and we may
picture labor (aided by the "waiting" function) as engaged in replacing a batch of potential consumers' goods
to take the place of the batch of consumers' goods that
is coming to fruition each year. The conditions represented in Case II may thus be diagramed as follows:

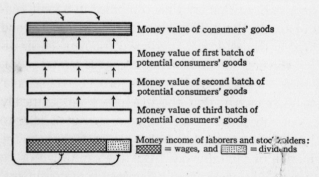

Money value of consumers' goods

Money value of first batch of
potential consumers' goods

Money value of second batch of
potential consumers' goods

Money value of third batch of
potential consumers' goods

Money income of laborers and stockholders:
▨▨▨ = wages, and ▦▦▦ = dividends

Here, again, a balance is struck between production
and consumption, between supply and demand, between the flow of money income into the hands of consumers (laborers and stockholders) and the money value

of the consumers' goods produced. In Case II the authors assume that goods worth $1,000,000 are purchased, that $900,000 are paid out in wages and $100,000 in dividends.

We now come to the third case presented by Foster and Catchings. Here we encounter for the first time the phenomenon of additional saving. In Case II we have assumed a certain amount of past saving, since there was available a certain amount of accumulated capital. But in Case II there was no *new* saving. The capital worn out each year (converted, as it were, into consumers' goods) was replaced by a new batch of capital. But the total volume of capital goods remained the same. In Case III, however, we have a fresh addition to the capital accumulation in the form of an inventory of unsold goods. This extra batch of goods is the result of the employment of an additional number of laborers. We may assume (without doing violence to the authors' argument) that these new goods are produced by the direct application of labor without the use of any fixed capital, thus leaving the former system of production (as pictured in Case II) intact. The authors of *Profits* assume that the same quantity of consumers' goods is sold as before, namely, $1,000,000 worth, and that $1,000,000 are paid out in wages ($900,000 to the old workers and $100,000 to the new). The wage-earners thus have a sufficient flow of money income to take off all the consumers' goods placed on the markets. In this case, however, no dividends are distributed, but, instead, the money ($100,000) is used to pay the new laborers. The former dividend receivers are now, of course, in no position to buy consumers' goods, but, instead, these goods are purchased by the new laborers. The stockholders do, however, receive something for the performance of their function, but their reward takes the form of an increase in the assets of the corporation — the unsold inventory of goods. Thus the equilibrium between the production of consumers' goods and the flow of money income into the hands of consumers is maintained, and supply equals demand. Case III may be diagramed as follows:

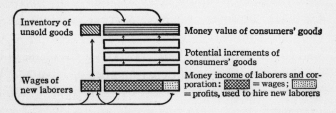

In Case IV the new goods produced by the additional laborers are sold, but not for money. Instead the corporation receives, in return for the sale of the goods, accounts receivable. In other words, the goods are sold on credit. The wage-earners, as before, are able to take off the old stock of consumers' goods, and since the new stock is being sold on credit, equilibrium again exists between production and consumption, between demand and supply. There is not a sufficient flow of money income into the hands of consumers, but the deficiency of money purchasing power is offset by the granting of credits and the accumulation of accounts receivable in the hands of the corporation. Case IV may be diagramed as follows:

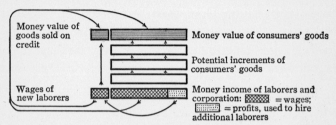

In Case V the situation is very similar to that obtaining in Cases III and IV, with the exception that the additional laborers are supposed to produce capital goods and not consumers' goods, as in the previous cases. Instead of the profits ($100,000) being distributed to stockholders, as in Case II, they are kept in the business, are used to employ additional laborers who are put to work (directly without the aid of machinery, we may assume for the sake of simplicity) to construct capital, or producers', goods. The profits of the corporation ($100,000) are carried to the surplus account, and the assets of the corporation are increased by a corresponding addition to its fixed capital equipment. The old laborers are still engaged as before in producing (by the roundabout method) consumers' goods amounting in money value to $1,000,000. These laborers are paid as before, $900,000. The total volume of wages paid to the old and new laborers is therefore $1,000,000, just enough to buy the $1,000,000 worth of consumers' goods produced. Since the stockholders are paid no dividends, they are not in a position to make any purchases, but content themselves by the fact that the net assets of the corporation have been increased. Equilibrium between the supply and the demand for consumers' goods is thus maintained. Case V may be diagramed as follows:

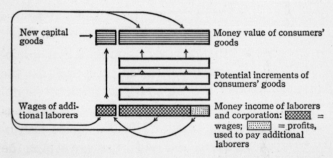

We now come to Case VI, a very important one. Here it is assumed that the additional capital goods, created as explained in Case V, are put to work to produce consumers' goods. For the sake of simplicity we shall assume that the rate of depreciation on this new capital is 100 per cent per annum. It is thus worn out in a year, and in the process gives off consumers' goods. We shall assume that the laborers who originally created this equipment are next employed to build a new batch of capital goods which will replace the batch worn out in the process of producing additional consumers' goods. We again assume that the

machinery is completely automatic and requires no
labor to tend it.

Case VI may be diagramed as follows:

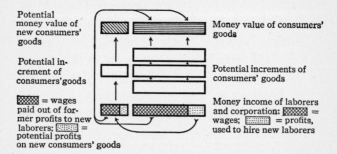

Potential
money value of
new consumers'
goods

Potential in-
crement of
consumers' goods

▨▨ = wages
paid out of for-
mer profits to new
laborers; ▦▦ =
potential profits
on new consumers' goods

Money value of consumers'
goods

Potential increments of
consumers' goods

Money income of laborers
and corporation: ▨▨ =
wages; ▦▦ = profits,
used to hire new laborers

In Case VI, then, we witness an enlarged output of
consumers' goods as a result of the employment of new
laborers, precisely as in Cases III and IV. The essential
difference between the former cases and the present one
is this: in Cases III and IV the *new* laborers were set
to work to produce consumers' goods directly, whereas
in Case VI they work indirectly *via the production of
capital goods.* Working by the roundabout, or capitalistic, method, the product should be greater than would
be possible by the direct method, and we should therefore expect them to produce goods worth (on the old
price basis) say $110,000. Foster and Catchings, how-
ever, assume the production to be exactly the same as
in Cases III and IV. But that would leave no profits
for the corporation in spite of the fact that an additional
investment is now made in fixed capital. In Cases III
and IV there was no investment, and hence we have

assumed (as have Foster and Catchings) that there were no profits, but that the value of the whole product was identical with the wages paid. To be strictly accurate this would, of course, not be the case. But no matter. The chief point to notice is that the value of the product of the new laborers should be greater in Case VI than in Cases III and IV owing to the use of machinery.

Case VI is again differentiated from Cases III and IV in that an effort is here made to sell the goods for cash. But since only $1,000,000 have been paid out in wages, and since no dividends have been distributed, it follows that the flow of money income into the hands of consumers is not sufficient to purchase the consumers' goods (worth $1,110,000) which have been produced. Hence the equilibrium between demand and supply is upset. If prices remain constant (as is at first assumed by the authors of *Profits*), the result is that a stock of unsold goods is left on the market, and if this process is continued year after year a larger and larger stock of unsold goods will appear. The crux of the matter is, the authors state, that money once used to bring about the production of goods is again used to bring about the production of goods before it is used to bring about the consumption of goods. "If we have come upon anything of major importance since we left our pioneer on the very first page, this may well be it."[1]

Let us pause here and take stock. What is the fundamental thing that has occurred? At first the cases in

[1] *Profits*, p. 279.

Profits appear involved, but in reality the matter is quite plain. What has occurred is simply this: A part of the old consumers (the stockholders) have refrained from consumption, have saved, have employed more laborers, and thus have increased the total output of consumers' goods. If these laborers are employed in the roundabout method (as in Case VI), the added value output is still greater than if they produced consumers' goods directly (or worked along with the old laborers by the aid of the old machinery). In the former case, however, the overproduction of consumers' goods would be postponed as long as they were engaged in constructing the new capital and until the new capital was put into operation to turn out consumers' goods.

It is to be noticed that the increased production has come about by means of the employment of additional laborers (working either directly or indirectly). But a similar result, different only in degree, would occur if additional capital were accumulated without employing more laborers. This aspect of the matter the authors of *Profits* have not considered. In a society in which some laborers were engaged in the replacement of capital goods and others in the production of consumers' goods, an addition to the capital equipment could be accomplished by withdrawing laborers from the production of consumers' goods and engaging them upon the production of producers' goods. This change in the currents of production may be accomplished in one of two ways: In the first place, the stockholders may voluntarily direct their demand from consumers' goods to producers' goods. In this event the equilibrium of consumer demand and consumer supply would not be upset until the new capital goods began to function. Consumer demand and consumer supply would both be reduced. In the second place, the corporation might *arbitrarily* decide to divert production from consumers' goods to producers' goods, without, however, curtailing its distribution of dividends. We suppose, moreover, that the stockholders would continue to purchase consumers' goods. The first effect of such a change in the currents of production would be a deficiency in the supply of consumers' goods coming on the markets, with no corresponding curtailment of consumer demand, since no change is assumed either in the amount of money paid out to wage-earners and stockholders or in the spending habits of these individuals. It follows that the demand for and supply of consumers' goods is upset, and the prices of consumers' goods will rise. The rise in prices comes about as a result of the effort of consumers to bid the limited supply away from each other. In the end, however, no consumer has been able to purchase as many goods as was possible before the corporation changed its production policy. The new capital goods which the corporation is making and accumulating are therefore being paid for out of the purchasing power which each consumer has lost through the rise in the prices of consumers' goods. The new capital is the product of the enforced saving imposed upon all consumers as a result of the changed production policy of the corporation and the consequent decline in the supply of consumers' goods.

But eventually the new capital goods will have been completed and will be utilized for the making of consumers' goods. The corporation's labor force is then equipped with more elaborate machinery, and so it follows that the total output of consumers' goods will exceed the production maintained under the old régime before the corporation began to add to its total capital equipment. The productive process has been made still more roundabout, more capitalistic than before, since there has been a net addition to the total capital equipment. As a result the final output of consumers' goods is increased. There has not, however, occurred any increase in the money income received by wage-earners and stockholders. The final result of the addition of the new capital equipment is therefore an oversupply of consumers' goods. The prices of consumers' goods will fall before a new equilibrium can be reached. Thus while the new capital equipment is being made, a deficiency of the supply of consumers' goods raises prices; but when the new capital goods begin to make consumers' goods, a deficiency of consumer demand relative to the supply of consumers' goods develops, and either a mass of unsold goods accumulates, or prices are forced even below the original level.[1] And,

[1] Compare with J. S. Mill, *Principles of Political Economy* (Ashley edition), pp. 67–68, 561.

as is well known, falling prices destroy the profit margin and put a damper on production.

Attention should again be called to the fact that the illustration immediately preceding is not derived from the cases presented in *Profits*. The illustration in *Profits* assumes that the new capital is made by *additional* laborers. Both cases, however, involve saving. Both appear to support the authors' contention that the process of corporate or individual saving inevitably creates a deficiency of consumer demand, resulting in either an accumulation of unsold goods or a fall in prices and consequent business depression, unless such deficiency can be made up in some other manner.

Corporations and individuals must necessarily save; yet saving creates a deficiency of consumer demand. This is the "dilemma of thrift," the most essential conclusion of *Profits*. It is contended by Foster and Catchings "that money spent is used *first* to take away consumers' goods, whereas in many cases money invested is used *first* to produce more consumers' goods. And when individual income is invested, and thus used twice in succession to bring goods to market, it creates a deficiency in purchasing power." [1] If consumers, instead of *spending* all their incomes, invest in corporation securities, and if the corporation disburses the money in the process of increasing production, consumers will still have just enough money to buy the original output,

---

[1] *Profits*, pp. 284–285. Compare with Marx, *Capital*, Vol. III, chap. xv.

but not enough to buy the additional output. "To prevent such a deficiency, to maintain the balance between production and consumption, and thus to make sustained prosperity possible, money which is used in the production of goods, must be used in the consumption of goods before it is again used in the production of goods, or the effect of such use on the annual equation must be offset in some way. In short, whenever money is used twice in succession to produce goods, as it is in many cases when individuals invest their incomes, it is doing its part, as our Cases show, to stock the market beyond the capacity of consumers to buy at current prices."[1]

This condition, they contend, is, however, brought about only when individuals save in certain ways.[2] They therefore raise two questions: (1) Which ways of saving cause deficiencies in purchasing power? (2) What proportion of individual incomes is saved in these ways?

The authors of *Profits* enumerate and discuss seven ways of saving: (1) in real estate, (2) in commodities, (3) in hoarded money, (4) in banks, (5) in life insurance, (6) in corporation securities, and (7) in government securities. The first in no way involves the production-consumption equation. The total volume of money in consumers' hands and the total volume of commodities in consumers' markets remain exactly as before. Nor

---

[1] *Profits*, p. 285.
[2] Compare and contrast with Hobson, *The Economics of Unemployment*.

does the second method cause a deficiency in purchasing power. But when these hoarded goods are later used up and current buying is correspondingly curtailed, a deficiency of consumer demand is created. Saving, in the form of consumable goods, is therefore likely to develop trouble eventually.[1] The third method, the hoarding of currency, causes a dollar deficiency in consumer purchasing power to the extent of the dollars hoarded.[2] Whether or not savings in banks, the fourth method, cause a deficiency in consumer buying depends on what the banks do with the money. If it is invested by the banks in such a way that it is used twice in succession for the production of goods, a deficiency is created. The authors believe that more than one half the savings deposits are so used. Likewise savings in life insurance, the fifth method, are invested in large part in production loans, and hence are used twice in succession in creating supply instead of being used alternately in creating and in absorbing the supply. Thus a deficiency of consumer purchasing power is created. The same argument applies to savings invested in corporate securities. Savings invested in government securities, the last method enumerated, are usually used by the government for consumption purposes, and so create no

[1] See also Arthur Spiethoff, "Krisen," *Handwörterbuch der Staatswissenschaften* (1925), VI, p. 74.

[2] This is Case VII. It assumes that cash savings are hoarded. Consumer purchasing power is correspondingly curtailed, and so consumer demand fails to keep pace with the supply of consumers' goods. This case is intended to show the effect of *hoarding*, as distinct from *saving*.

deficiency of consumer demand.[1] Thus the conclusion is reached that if people do not spend all their income, there is a deficiency in consumer demand unless the effect of their savings is offset in some other way.

Now before going any farther, it may be well to state at this point that a similar deficiency of consumer demand might occur for numberless other reasons besides the one here discussed; namely, an increase in capital goods or saving. In fact, all that the authors have shown is that if the production of consumers' goods is increased, and if there has not at the same time occurred an increase in the flow of money income into the hands of consumers, overproduction and falling prices will ensue.

Let us suppose that new natural resources are discovered. There follows an increased output of goods even though no additional saving takes place. Assuming no change in the volume of circulating media, or the amount of money income flowing into the hands of consumers, the demand for these goods fails to keep pace with the supply. Either there will develop an inventory of unsold goods or prices will fall.

A precisely similar situation will develop in each of the following cases (among many others that might be cited), as can readily be seen without further argument : (1) increased personal efficiency of labor, (2) improved management methods, (3) new inventions and improved processes, (4) increased population and labor supply.

[1] Cf. Malthus, *Principles of Political Economy*, p. 395.

The last-named situation perhaps needs brief comment. More laborers will be applied to the old resources and capital equipment, the total output of consumers' goods will be increased, though the average product will probably be lower. Consumers' *wants* and *needs* will increase even faster than the production of consumers' goods; but consumer *demand* (in money terms) will not increase at all, since with the same volume of circulating media the flow of money into the hands of consumers will be no greater than before. Thus there must develop a supply of unsold goods, or else prices will fall.

Moreover, while Foster and Catchings are quite right in assuming that an increase in capital equipment will eventually result in an increased supply of consumers' goods, in the opposite direction attention may be called to the fact that the failure to replace capital goods, and the utilization of capital-replacing labor to produce consumers' goods, may temporarily (until the old capital goods are used up) result in an increase in the supply of consumers' goods. Saving will *eventually* result in an increased output of consumers' goods, but, on the other hand, a society may temporarily increase its current output of consumers' goods by eating up its capital supply.[1] Any sudden increase or decrease of capital accumulation and saving *tends* to upset the equilibrium of demand and supply.

[1] Cf. H. B. Hastings. *Costs and Profits*, chap. v. Houghton Mifflin Company.

It will be seen from the foregoing that there is no more reason to suppose that thrift and capital accumulation will eventually upset the equilibrium of consumer supply and demand than many other dynamic factors. If we must assume, as do the authors of *Profits* in the cases cited, that the flow of money income into the hands of consumers remains unchanged, then it must follow that *any change* in the productive process which increases the output of consumers' goods will upset the equilibrium of consumer demand and supply. If it is correct to say that thrift and saving will inevitably develop an overstocked market, then the same must be said of the discovery of new natural resources, of an increase in population, an advance in the arts, or an increase in personal efficiency.

But now why assume that the "money" supply is fixed. Everyone knows that it actually is not. And this Foster and Catchings admit. They therefore withdraw this artificial assumption and proceed to ask the question May not the deficiency of consumer demand be offset by an increase in the circulating media?

In Case X[1] additional bank credit is issued amounting to $90,000. These loans are made to manufacturers,

---

[1] In Cases VIII and IX the authors withdraw their original assumption that the price level remains unchanged, and show the effect of a decline in the price level resulting from the failure of consumer demand. They argue that if prices of all sorts fell simultaneously, synchronized, continued production at a profit would be possible. They show, however, that prices do not move in this fashion; that there are lags that destroy the profit margin.

who use the added funds to employ additional laborers (over and above the number employed in Case II) in order to increase production. Case X [1] may be diagramed as follows:

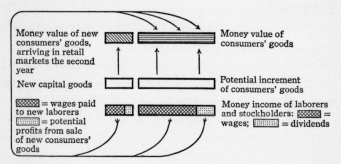

During the first year the new laborers are building new capital equipment. Only in the second year do the new consumers' goods finally arrive in the retail markets. Until the new capital goods finally begin to turn out consumers' goods, consumer demand will outrun the supply of consumers' goods, since the former has increased by $90,000 (the amount of the new bank credit created), whereas the latter, for the time being, is no greater than before. Accordingly, the prices of consumers' goods will rise until a new equilibrium is reached between demand and supply.

But now what will happen the following year, when the new consumers' goods begin to arrive in the retail

[1] In Case X we have assumed, for the sake of simplicity, that all capital equipment is worn out in one year, whereas in Case II the depreciation period is three years.

markets? We now find that the supply of consumers' goods more than matches the additional consumer demand. Ten per cent more laborers were added, and so the wage bill was increased 10 per cent; that is, from $900,000 to $990,000. But the original money value (see Case II) of the former supply of consumers' goods was $1,000,000, the extra $100,000 being paid out in dividends. The new consumers' goods should likewise sell at a figure that would yield a profit. If the old laborers produced a product worth more than their wages, the new laborers should likewise. If the new laborers and the new capital which they produce are assumed to be as productive as the old, the total increase in the physical output of consumers' goods should be 10 per cent. But we have seen that the money income paid out to wage-earners and stockholders did not increase 10 per cent but only 9 per cent. Thus the supply of consumers' goods has increased more than the increase in the flow of money income compared with the condition obtaining before the new bank credit was issued. The prices of consumers' goods will therefore fall from the high level reached during the first year of the expansion to a point even below that which obtained prior to the disturbance of the old equilibrium.

Now suppose, however, that still more bank credit is issued. Another $90,000 of loans are made and credited to the deposit accounts of business men. With these added funds they employ an additional group of laborers. This brings us to Case XI. The total wages paid are now $1,080,000. Add to this the $100,000 dividends, and you have a total consumer demand of $1,180,000, or an increase of 18 per cent. The consumers' goods which were in process of being produced (via the production of capital goods) during the first year of the expansion emerge in the second year and are placed in the retail market together with the former annual supply. This makes an increase in the supply of consumers' goods of 10 per cent. Relative to the preëxpansion period, therefore, consumer demand has outrun consumer supply; but relative to the preceding year — the first year of the expansion — the increase in consumer demand has not kept pace with the increase in consumer supply, and so the price level falls below the high point reached in the first expansion year. This is evident from the fact that in the first year of expansion consumer demand stood at 109, and consumer supply at 100, relative to the preëxpansion period. In the second year, as we have shown, consumer demand stands at 118 and consumer supply at 110. Foster and Catchings conclude that the higher price-level which first results from an increase in the volume of "money" cannot be sustained, so long as production expands, unless the volume of money is increased at an accelerating rate.[1]

[1] As a matter of fact, the authors' illustration does not consider a uniform *rate* of increase, but only an equivalent *absolute* increase. A uniform *rate* of increase would, however, give the same conclusion, the difference being only one of degree. The real point is that as the volume of consumers' goods created increases 10 per cent per annum, consumers' incomes increase only 9 per cent per annum.

This brings us to Case XII. Here we return to the conditions obtaining in Case X during the first year of expansion. Suppose, now, that in the subsequent year the corporation repays its loan of $90,000 at the bank. The new laborers are discharged, and consumer demand falls back to the relative figure 100, the same as in the preëxpansion period. But during this second year the new consumers' goods emerge and are placed in the retail markets. Consumer supply therefore equals 110. Obviously the equilibrium is disturbed, and the price level will fall 10 points or so below the preëxpansion level.

What do these cases show? They show, the authors tell us, that an expansion of circulating media by means of an issue of bank credit will not in the long run offset any deficiency of consumer demand arising out of such an increase in the supply of consumers' goods as was assumed in Cases III to VI. In fact, the issue of bank credit itself sets up a chain of reactions which will eventually result in a deficiency of consumer demand. Thus instead of offsetting any deficiency created by saving, it tends itself to develop a deficiency of consumer demand.

The manner in which the money is used is of prime importance. A balance must be maintained between money *used to buy goods and money used to produce goods*. If the "increase of money is too large on the producers' side, the result is an output of goods beyond the capacity of consumers to buy them. If, on the other hand, the increase of money is too great on the consumers' side, the result is a bidding up of prices which in the ordinary course of business also culminates in overproduction." [1]

Supply and demand are indeed always equal in a barter economy. Overproduction — a supply in excess of demand — is held to be a purely monetary phenomenon. "Money is suspended purchasing power, left hanging over the markets to be used nobody knows *when*, or *where*, or for *what*. The sale of goods for money, therefore, creates the new possibility of a demand without supply, or a supply without demand." [2]

Two erroneous assumptions, the authors tell us, are commonly made : (1) "that the goods produced and the credit created correspond dollar for dollar," and (2) "that the new goods and the new credit affect the markets at the same time." [3] The cases presented show that an increased output of money "at first yield consumers more than enough money, and presently far less than enough money, to buy the available goods at the current price-level." [4] "The fact that all the goods belong to some one does not mean that some one receives the money income capable of buying them." [5] The "time inevitably comes in a period of expanding production when the *total* flow of money to consumers does not keep pace with the flow of goods." [6]

Bank loans are used principally to increase production

[1] *Profits*, p. 318.   [4] Ibid. p. 320.
[2] Ibid. p. 320.   [5] Ibid. p. 321.
[3] Ibid. p. 320.   [6] Ibid. p. 321.

rather than to increase consumption. When they are invested in new capital facilities the first effect, it is true, is an increase in consumers' purchasing power. But investments in new capital facilities are made for the purpose of creating goods that can be sold at a profit; and if this expectation is realized, the result is a deficiency of consumers' purchasing power. Thus the first effect of new bank loans used in production is to bring new money into consumers' markets in advance of new commodities, and this "raises prices, makes the business outlook seem better than it is, and creates overconfidence." [1] After a while the expansion of bank credit for the purpose of production "increases the means of producing commodities out of proportion to the means of buying them." [2]

The authors have so far taken no account of government taxes and expenditures. They now raise the question whether or not these operations in any way offset the deficiency of consumer demand. Their conclusion is that, in so far as government expenditures are financed by means of taxes and loans which do not involve an expansion of the volume of money in circulation, these operations do not offset in any degree the deficiencies in purchasing power which are caused by private industry.

The following quotation gives a concise summary of the conclusion reached by the authors:

[1] *Profits*, p. 325.   [2] Ibid. p. 325.

It is an amazing fact, however, that consumption cannot
long keep the pace since, as industry is now financed and
corporate savings are now effected, the flow of money to
consumers does not long keep pace with the flow of goods ;
and without a full flow of *money* into consumption there
cannot be a full flow of *goods* into consumption. The
necessary flow of money is not sustained because, when
the output is enlarged, producers do not disburse to consumers, directly or indirectly, an amount of money equal
to the final sales price of their products. This failure of
industry to provide consumers with enough money to
buy its products is inherent in the profit system, for all
payments by industry to consumers are advances made
with the expectation of recovering from consumers all that
has been advanced, with profits in addition. As business expands and profits are thus realized, approximately half the
profits are used to produce more goods. In fact, it is the
established, approved, and, under the present system
the necessary, practice of the various industries to dis-
tribute only part of the realized profits and to use the
rest, in one way or another, to increase capital. Thus the
flow of goods which consumers must buy if business is to
prosper increases more rapidly than the flow of money
to consumers.

Furthermore, even if producers disbursed all their
profits and all other incomes, and even if they acted
promptly enough — which is impossible since profits
cannot be distributed until after they are realized — there
would still be a deficiency of consumer buying; for consumers must save, and usually they save in ways which increase the output of industry. Thus a part of the corporate
income which is received from consumers and returned to

them, as wages, rent, interest, and dividends, is used by them not to purchase goods, but to bring about the production of more goods; and every dollar which is thus saved instead of spent increases the initial deficiency. . . .

Both producers and consumers must save. Since, however, it is consumption and not abstinence that stimulates production, neither producers nor consumers are able to save without to some extent frustrating the social object of saving. This is what we have called the dilemma of thrift.[1]

The deficiency in consumer purchasing power is not made up from "additions to the money in circulation, because these additions, originating as they do principally on the producer side, and being used to turn out goods to be sold at a profit, lead presently to increases in goods which exceed the increases in purchasing power." [2]

The leading conclusions of Foster and Catchings may then be stated as follows:

1. If bank credit is expanded for purposes of increased production, the flow of consumer demand will increase before there is any increase in the volume of consumers' goods. This is due to the fact that production takes time. The productive factors employed are paid while the productive process is going on, but the product is not completed for several months or perhaps even years. In the meantime consumer demand outruns consumer supply, and prices rise.

[1] William T. Foster and Waddill Catchings, *Profits*, pp. 399–401. Houghton Mifflin Company.
[2] Ibid. p. 401.

This analysis, is, we believe, sound for certain phases of the business cycle, but it contributes nothing new, as we shall see later, to the theory of the business cycle, nor does it grapple with the forces that underlie these movements.

2. Unless bank credit is issued at an accelerated *rate*, consumer supply will outrun consumer demand as soon as the new batch of consumers' goods begin to be poured on the market. As a result, prices fall. This conclusion is based on the assumption that consumer income (and therefore demand) is increased at a rate corresponding to the ratio of the increased *outlay* (expenses incurred in expanding production) to the former consumers' income, whereas consumers' supply is increased at a rate corresponding to the ratio of the added expense outlay to the former expense outlay. Or, to put it in *absolute* terms, rather than in terms *of rate of increase*, the conclusion is based on the assumption that the absolute increase in consumer money income (or demand) is equal to the added expense outlay, whereas the absolute increase in consumers' supply (measured in terms of money) is equal to the added expense outlay *plus profit*.

The assumption is that a 10 per cent increase in expenses will employ 10 per cent more productive factors and eventually result in a 10 per cent increase in product. But since a 10 per cent increase in expenses will only add 9 per cent to consumers' incomes (assuming that the expenses of production constitute 90 per cent of the total value output, the remaining 10 per cent being profits),[1] it follows that consumers' supply will outrun consumers' demand, and prices will fall.

This statement of the case suggests a point which contributes to an understanding of the business cycle, but the manner in which it is stated by Foster and Catchings leads, as the present writer sees it, to wrong conclusions.

3. If increased output is financed out of corporate and individual savings (instead of by bank credit), consumers' demand will remain equal to the flow of consumers' goods so long as the new production is in process; but when the new finished products are at last turned out, the supply of consumers' goods will exceed consumers' demand, and prices will fall unless offset by an expansion of bank credit. But, as we have seen, Foster and Catchings contend that such an expansion of bank credit even though issued at precisely the right time could at best only defer the failure of consumers' demand. This follows, it is claimed, from the argument presented in (2) above, to the effect that bank credit is issued mainly to producers and therefore eventually results in consumer supply outrunning consumer demand.

It follows that it is impossible for society to save without producing price fluctuations, prosperity, and depression. This the present writer believes is not true. We shall show later that a uniform rate of saving is con-

[1] The words "expenses" and "profits" are here used in the business, or accounting, sense.

sistent with a stable economic equilibrium; that the disruption of this equilibrium is not due to the fact of saving per se, but to dynamic forces inherent in a progressive industrial order which carries on production by means of the capitalistic, or roundabout, method in a highly complex money and exchange economy.

We conclude, then, that the argument advanced in *Profits*, reduced to its lowest terms, amounts to this: Consumer demand and consumer supply must remain equal, or the prices of consumers' goods will rise or fall. A rise in prices stimulates industry, and a fall in prices brings depression. Consumer demand runs in terms of money. It varies with the money income flowing into the hands of consumers and the per cent of this income used by them to buy consumers' goods. Consumer supply varies with the consumers' goods flowing into the retail markets. Anything that upsets the equilibrium between consumer demand and consumer supply will start industry on the up-grade of prosperity or the down-grade of depression, as the case may be. A change in the production of consumers' goods unaccompanied by a simultaneous change in the money demand for consumers' goods would disturb the equilibrium.

This skeleton statement of the conditions necessary for economic equilibrium is satisfactory as far as it goes, but it is too simple for an adequate analysis of the complex forces at work in the business cycle. However, taking it as it stands, it is pertinent to show that the authors have overlooked many factors that would disturb the equilibrium they have sketched. They have limited their discussion to the effect of saving and the issue of bank credit on consumer demand and consumer supply. But there may be other disturbing factors, such as an increase in the labor supply, a discovery of new natural resources, invention and scientific discoveries, improved management processes, increased personal efficiency of the population, and a prodigal eating up of past capital accumulations.

On the other hand, they have not taken sufficient account of the continuity of the modern production process and the equilibrating forces.

It is not the purpose of this chapter, however, to discuss *Profits* critically, but merely to state and analyze the main arguments presented by the authors. In a later chapter we shall examine their theory in the light of the literature pertaining to the business cycle.

CHAPTER IV

THE CAPITALISTIC PROCESS OF PRODUCTION AS CAUSE OF THE BUSINESS CYCLE

In Chapter II we have considered a group of writers who find the disturbing factors which upset the economic equilibrium, and so produce the business cycle, in the manner in which, under the capitalistic order, the income is distributed. This theory, as we have seen, aroused the Say-Ricardo-Mill school, which developed the so-called law of markets. This law in essence means that a nation's purchasing power is not affected by the *manner* in which income is distributed but solely by the national product; that the manner in which income is distributed only affects the *direction of demand* but not the totality of demand; that the manner in which income is distributed will therefore only affect the kinds of things produced but not the totality of production.[1] *Changes* in income distribution would, it is true, bring

---

[1] From the long-run point of view, the classicals did not hold that total production is unaffected by the distribution of income, since the distribution of income affects the accumulation of capital. Moreover, it is to be noted, as George Gunton pointed out (*Wealth and Progress* (1887), pp. 8, 30, 268, 278), that a more equal distribution of income, giving greater purchasing power to the masses, tends in the direction of mechanized, large-scale production. In this respect the physical output is therefore likely to be greater if the income is more equally distributed. Thus the *direction of demand* itself affects the *totality of demand*.

about shifts in production to meet the changes in demand. Sudden changes in income distribution would indeed disturb the smooth equilibrium of production, but the disturbance would consist of the difficulties inherent in adjusting the productive factors to the new demand situation; in shifting from low-profit industries to high-profit industries.

The capitalistic-distribution theory of the business cycle ran its course particularly in the second and fourth quarters of the nineteenth century, periods of falling prices and apparently glutted markets. The voices of the adherents of this school are still heard, but, in the main, with the new note struck by such writers as Foster and Catchings or P. W. Martin. The Say-Sismondi-Malthus-Ricardo debate was increasingly seen to be barren of results. The Say-Ricardo school, while fundamentally sound, left the problem unsolved. As has so frequently been true of economic generalizations, it tackled the problem in terms of long-run tendencies, which in effect meant that it refused to recognize it as a problem at all. On the other hand, the Lauderdale-Malthus-Sismondi solution is logically untenable to anyone who will take the pains to think the problem through to the end.

At the turn of the century the approach to the problem shifted from the side of distribution to the side of production. The new school attacked the problem not from the standpoint of social institutions but from the standpoint of the material conditions of production in the modern capitalistic order. The controlling factors were sought not in the juristic framework of society but in the technological conditions of the capitalistic, or roundabout, method of production.

Karl Marx, while following in the main the Lauderdale-Malthus-Sismondi doctrine, nevertheless in Vol. II, Part II, chap. ix, of *Capital*, suggests a capitalistic-production theory of the economic cycle. The statement referred to in Marx is as follows:

To the same extent that the volume of the value and the duration of the fixed capital develop with the evolution of the capitalistic mode of production, does the life of industry and of industrial capital develop in each particular investment into one of many years, say of ten years on an average. If the development of fixed capital extends the length of this life on one side, it is on the other side shortened by the continuous revolution of the instruments of production, which likewise increases incessantly with the development of capitalist production. This implies a change in the instruments of production and the necessity of continuous replacement on account of virtual wear and tear, long before they are worn out physically. One may assume that this life cycle, in the essential branches of great industry, now averages ten years. However, it is not a question of any one definite number here. So much at least is evident that this cycle comprising a number of years, through which capital is compelled to pass by its fixed part, furnishes a material basis for the periodical commercial crises in which business goes through successive periods of lassitude, average activity, overspeeding, and crisis. It is true that the periods in which capital is in-

vested are different in time and place. But a crisis is always
the starting point of a large amount of new investments.
Therefore it also constitutes, from the point of view of
society, more or less of a new material basis for the next
cycle of turnover.[1]

The suggestion here made by Marx is that the life
cycle of fixed capital is at the root of the periodic
industrial cycle.

The real founder of the Çapitalistic Production school
is, however, not Marx, but Tougan-Baranowsky,[2] who
put forth the view that the prosperity phase of the cycle
is characterized by the augmentation of the demand for
the means of production; depression, by the decline of
this demand. In the ascending phase new industrial
enterprises are constructed in large quantities.[3] In his
French edition Baranowsky quotes Llewellyn Smith's
testimony before the Parliamentary Committee on Distress from Want of Employment (1895), as saying:

The periodic fluctuations are particularly strong in the
industrial branches, such as the construction of ships, the

[1] *Capital* (Kerr edition), Vol. II, p. 211.

[2] M. Tougan-Baranowsky published the first Russian edition of his
work in 1894; the German edition appeared in 1901, and the French
edition, *Les Crises industrielles en Angleterre*, appeared in 1913. The
French edition was used by the present writer.

According to Jean Lescure (*Crises générales et périodiques de surproduction* (1923), pp. 358–360) it was Tougan-Baranowsky who gave the
first impulse in the new direction, though he received his inspiration
from Marx.

[3] M. Tougan-Baranowsky, *Les Crises industrielles en Angleterre*, p. 253.
M. Giard & É. Brière.

construction of machines and other analogous branches which Walter Bagehot has called the "instrumental trades." The whole of the national production varies only a little from year to year, but these feeble variations suffice to provoke violent oscillations in the industrial branches which furnish the means of production.[1]

On the other hand, the increased production of fixed capital, through the interdependence of industries, results in a general augmentation of the demand for all goods.[2]

Now what causes these cycles in the production of fixed capital? According to Baranowsky the cause is to be found in the periodic accumulation of large masses of loan capital, which forces itself into the production of fixed capital, and this brings on a period of prosperity. Eventually these accumulated savings are exhausted, the production of fixed capital declines, and depression ensues. "The loanable capital accumulates without interruption, but it transforms itself into productive capital only by spurts."[3] Even though depression brings reduced incomes to entrepreneurs and laborers, still, because of the increase in the real incomes of the salaried and creditor classes, the accumulation of loanable funds goes on at a considerable rate during this phase of the cycle. The accumulation of loanable funds, or free capital, is therefore more regular than the production of fixed capital. The prosperity phase of the cycle is characterized by the transformation of free

[1] Tougan-Baranowsky, op. cit., p. 257.   [2] Ibid. p. 258.   [3] Ibid. p. 261.

capital into fixed capital; the depression phase, by an accumulation of free, mobile capital.[1]

The transformation of loanable funds into productive capital requires a certain proportionality in the distribution of free capital between the different branches of production. But the accumulated free capital can find no outlet into productive capital. When the moment arrives in which the accumulated loanable funds can find an opening and can thus be converted into productive capital, then a new period of prosperity has commenced.[2]

The accumulated loanable funds (which rest, for example, as deposits in a bank and are not employed by the bank itself in loans) represent a latent purchasing power. This purchasing power, which accumulates during the bad years, does not exercise any influence upon the commodity market as long as the loanable funds are not placed. But when, for one reason or another, these funds find a placement, then latent purchasing power is transformed into effective purchasing power. The funds are spent and new productive capital is created, which increases the demand for the means of production and also for the objects of consumption. Industry finds a new market, created through the extension of production itself, and this extension is caused by the expenditure of the loanable funds which before remained inactive in the reserves of the banks.[3]

[1] Tougan-Baranowsky, op. cit. pp. 261–262. Baranowsky calls attention to John Stuart Mill's theory that it is the low interest rate consequent upon the pressure of funds which provokes a period of feverish speculation.   [2] Ibid. p. 263.   [3] Ibid. p. 264.

Bit by bit the previously accumulated loan capital is used up. Each entrepreneur finds it possible to use all the capital he can procure. The extraordinary extension of credit so characteristic of the prosperity phase of the cycle denotes an intensive demand for capital. The high rate of interest which one observes at the end of this period is a certain indication of the scarcity of loanable funds.[1]

Industrial prosperity is born of the expenditure of the loanable capital (representing latent purchasing power) which accumulated during the preceding years. The expenditure of loan capital results in the creation of new fixed capital. But finally the new equipment is finished. The building of new enterprises slows down. The demand for all the raw materials going into fixed capital declines. The distribution of production ceases to be proportional. Machines are less in demand. But the producers of fixed capital find it difficult to curtail production. Inactive capital is unable to pay interest. There follows an overproduction. The various industrial branches being dependent upon each other, this *partial* overproduction leads to a *general* overproduction. Prices fall; we enter the period of depression. The equilibrium of demand and supply is broken. As the new enterprises created a demand not only for fixed capital but also for objects of consumption for the workers, there follows, with the cessation of new capital construction, not only an overproduction in the branches of

[1] Ibid. pp. 264–265.

industry which furnish producers' goods but also in those which furnish consumption goods. This general overproduction is due to the lack of proportionality between the different branches of production. The monetary and credit difficulties are only secondary phenomena which result from the lack of proportionality.[1]

The capitalistic mechanism by which the periodic accumulation of loan capital is subsequently exhausted in the creation of new productive capital, is compared by Baranowsky to the working of a steam engine. The accumulation of loanable funds plays the rôle of the steam in the cylinder. When the pressure of the steam upon the piston attains a certain force, the piston is forced into motion and is pushed to the end of the cylinder. The steam escapes, and the piston returns to its former position. So the accumulated loanable capital acts upon industry. When it has reached a certain volume, industry is set in motion. Finally the funds are exhausted, and industry returns to its former condition.[2]

In the capitalistic economy consumption no longer commands production, but, on the contrary, production regulates consumption. The industrial cycle is determined not by the laws of consumption but by those of production. It is not because consumption increases

[1] Tougan-Baranowsky, op. cit. pp. 270–272.
[2] Ibid. p. 273. This illustration has become classic and is cited by many authors. Cf. E. H. Vogel, *Die Theorie des volkswirtschaftlichen Entwickelungsprozesses und das Krisenproblem*, p. 386; Jean Lescure, op. cit. pp. 367–368; A. C. Pigou, *Economics of Welfare*, p. 810.

that prosperity develops. On the contrary, the increase in consumption springs from the extension of production, and this from the rapid accumulation of capital, which in turn springs from the unequal division of social income. It is the inadequate remuneration of the working classes that is the fundamental cause of that rapid accumulation of capital which provokes the economic cycle.[1] In this manner Tougan-Baranowsky sought to reconcile his position with that of Lauderdale, Malthus, and Marx. Baranowsky thus occupies an intermediate stage between the Capitalistic Distribution school and the Capitalistic Production school.[2]

The first clear-cut representative of the Capitalistic Production school is not Tougan-Baranowsky but Arthur Spiethoff. Tougan-Baranowsky's *Studien zur Theorie und Geschichte der Handelskrisen in England*

---

[1] But the question may be asked, What has the *volume* of savings to do with the *cyclical* accumulation of capital? Why, asks Spiethoff, does not this accumulation proceed uniformly? Why is there first a period in which large masses of loan capital are piled up without being invested, followed by a period of "stormy investment"? Cf. Arthur Spiethoff, *Jahrbuch für Gesetzgebung, Verwaltung und Volkswirtschaft*, 1903, p. 696.

[2] It should be noted that with Tougan-Baranowsky it is the rapid accumulation of *loan* capital which breeds prosperity. During the prosperity period the *loan* capital is being exhausted, but the construction of *real* capital is going on apace. Prosperity is brought to a close because of the shortage of *loan* capital, while at the same time there is an oversupply of *real* capital. This explains the apparent inconsistency between Tougan-Baranowsky and the Capitalistic Distribution school.

Tougan-Baranowsky could also be grouped with the Exchange Economy school, since he emphasizes the interdependence of industries and the planlessness of the modern order. Cf. Baranowsky, op. cit. pp. 257–258; Spiethoff, op. cit. pp. 684–687; Lescure, op. cit. p. 358.

(Jena, 1901) served as a starting point [1] for Spiethoff in his "Vorbemerkungen," [2] a lecture given on December 17, 1901. In his "Die Krisentheorien von M. v. Tougan-Baranowsky und L. Pohle" (*Jahrbuch für Gesetzgebung*, 1903), Spiethoff refers to Tougan-Baranowsky's work as the first scientific monograph on crises.

With Spiethoff the causes of overproduction are to be found not in a wide chasm between supply and demand in the present economic system, but in special causes born of the mechanism of prosperity. Prosperity begins in especially hopeful branches in which capital expects unusual profits, and from these there is developed a general impetus. First, existing production plants are brought into full use. There follows the second stage, in which new plants are built. These new plants swallow up a large volume of investment capital and constructional raw materials of different kinds. But while this construction is going on there is no counterbalancing output of finished goods. In the third stage of the cycle the new plants begin to turn out finished products.[3] Finally, the "last period is the reverse of the second; a feverishly increased production throws its products on the market without being met by a like consumption." [4]

[1] Tougan-Baranowsky in his French edition (p. 277, note) refers to his earlier work as the point of departure for the studies of Spiethoff, Pohle, and others, who, he says, adopted it in whole or in part.

[2] Spiethoff, "Vorbemerkungen zu einer Theorie der Überproduktion," *Jahrbuch für Gesetzgebung*, 1902.

[3] Compare with Foster and Catchings.

[4] Spiethoff, op. cit. p. 730.

Newly opened up territory, new inventions in the old territory, require a large investment of fixed capital. Production stands before a great vacuum that needs to be filled. After some years of prosperity the empty vessel is filled, and then it is only a question of keeping the "stream aflowing"; and so, in spite of the rather steady consumers' demand, an end to the progressive development of industry is reached. He who today buys a machine or builds a house or a factory does not, like the man who buys a loaf of bread, have to repeat the performance tomorrow, but perhaps in ten or more years.

The production of equipment is conditioned by an investment of capital. At the beginning of a period of prosperity a very large mass of capital, gathered during the depression, is available for investment. This mass is being added to continually, but nevertheless all the time being absorbed. Eventually the time is reached when production can no longer lean back on the gatherings of depression but must look to new capital accumulation.[1]

At the beginning, then, of the fourth stage of the cycle the production of fixed capital has grown beyond the prevailing needs and also beyond the available investment-seeking capital. Through this cause the production of fixed capital is undermined. With the curtailment of the production of fixed capital there follows an unavoidable pressure on consumers' incomes, for both

[1] Spiethoff, op. cit. pp. 730–733; see also Spiethoff, "Krisen," *Handwörterbuch der Staatswissenschaften* (1925), VI, p. 74.

the profits of the employer and the reward of labor will decline. With the resulting worsening of incomes consumption is injured. Underconsumption follows from the fact that certain parts of the productive processes stand still. The influence spreads from the industries affected to other industries, and so general overproduction develops. In the ensuing depression new undertakings are looked upon with suspicion, and the possessors of capital will rather let their stores lie idle or be satisfied with small interest than take steps toward investment in fixed capital.[1]

The fall in the rate of profit and the low reward of labor reduce consumption, the decreasing consumption lowers prices, the fall in prices reduces production still further, the curtailment in production diminishes again the reward of labor and the rate of profit. There arises a formal vicious circle, and the interdependent effect of the different lines of industry on one another nourishes and increases the tendency to depression.[2]

During depression the chief problem confronting the industrialist is that of reducing costs through increased productivity and labor-saving machinery. But these improvements intensify depression. Many plants lose their value because of the new technique. The labor-saving machinery may either displace workers or press many skilled workers into the ranks of the unskilled.[3]

---

[1] Spiethoff, "Vorbemerkungen," pp. 737–738.
[2] Ibid. p. 741.
[3] Ibid. pp. 741–742.

During prosperity the income distribution does not affect the general consumption, for even though a part of the consumer income flows into the hands of the people who will not immediately consume all of it but change it in part into capital, still it is not lost to consumption. But in depression the unequal division of incomes does affect the overproduction, for then such part of the income as is saved is lost to consumption, since it is not used reproductively but is gathered in great idle masses of loan capital.[1]

Every limitation of production weakens afresh the buying and consuming power and is therefore a cause of the spread of the overproduction into new territory. It is therefore of the greatest importance that the production be kept up as far as possible and not reduced except for the most pressing causes. It may be more profitable for the entrepreneur to sell a smaller quantity for higher prices rather than a greater quantity for lower prices, but the general overproduction will be increased thereby. This is a case where the individual entrepreneur's interest in special branches is opposed to

[1] Ibid. p. 743. This argument calls to mind the "impair-savings" argument of N. Johannsen; cf. *Neglected Point in Connection with Crises* (1908) and *Business Depressions, their Cause* (1925). There is, however, this difference: Johannsen contends that depression savings are used to purchase the property of bankrupt employers and needy workmen, who use the funds so derived for consumption purposes. But on this basis there should be no reduction in purchasing power except for the prevailing unemployment, which then requires separate explanation. Cf. also Lauderdale, op. cit. p. 248. See also Spiethoff, "Krisen," *Handwörterbuch der Staatswissenschaften* (1925), VI, p. 80.

the general interest and where the Kartell works out to the injury of industry in general.[1]

With Spiethoff, then, the "real difference between prosperity and depression consists in the increasing or decreasing of the production of fixed capital and in the decreasing or increasing store of investment seeking capital."[2]

According to Spiethoff there is no reason to doubt that people will gradually be able to adjust themselves to the capitalistic process of production. The history of crises teaches that its character has largely changed, that we have overcome many "children's diseases" of the capitalistic manner of production.[3]

Gustav Cassel,[4] the distinguished Swedish economist, has carried forward the analysis started by Tougan-Baranowsky and Spiethoff. With Cassel a "period of advance is one of special increase in the production of fixed capital; a period of decline or a depression is one in which this production falls below the point it had reached."[5] The "essence of a conjuncture consists in an extraordinary production of fixed capital and a subsequent rapid decline of the same."[6] The "change

[1] Spiethoff, "Vorbemerkungen," p. 745. Cf. J. M. Clark, "Some Social Aspects of Overhead Costs," *American Economic Review* Supplement, March, 1923.

[2] Spiethoff, op. cit. p. 753.

[3] Ibid. pp. 756–758.

[4] Gustav Cassel, *The Theory of Social Economy.* Harcourt, Brace and Company, 1923.

[5] Ibid. p. 521.

[6] Ibid. p. 529. See also A. C. Pigou, *Industrial Fluctuations*, pp. 16–19. Macmillan & Company, Limited.

from periods of advance to periods of decline is in its innermost nature a variation in the production of fixed capital, but is not directly connected with the rest of production." [1]

But this is true only of the business cycle during, say, the last seventy-five years. Only after 1870 was the modern system of exchange and production definitely developed. By 1870 the older forms and causes of crises had substantially disappeared and the modern type of crises emerged. Before 1870 there were crises due to ignorance in the handling of coinage and note issues; misuse of state credit; speculative manipulations in the early days of joint-stock companies; colonization, together with the speculative trade and shifts in production growing therefrom; transition from manual labor to machine production; crop fluctuations (of major importance at a time when agriculture was predominant); occasional disturbances caused by changes in fashion or by wars. Hence Cassel thinks it premature to conceive of all crises and business cycles as necessary concomitants of the modern productive and social order. [2]

It is the *modern* conjuncture movement (business cycle), then, which is associated with the production of fixed capital. [3] And the two most important forms of

[1] Cassel, op. cit. p. 523. See also George H. Hull, *Industrial Depressions* (1911); T. E. Burton, *Financial Crises* (1902); and A. C. Pigou, op. cit. pp. 18–19.

[2] Cassel, op. cit. p. 507.

[3] Ibid. p. 519.

fixed capital are buildings and railways. Now from the
seventies iron has become the basic material for the
production of fixed capital. "The annual production of
iron may be taken as a measure of the annual production
of fixed capital." [1]

While the production of fixed capital varies with
"conjuncture movements," the production of consumption goods has little or no relation to these movements.
Coal is used largely (though not exclusively) for consumption purposes, and its production fluctuates much
less than the production of iron. The tonnage of capital
goods and other goods on German railways is given by
Cassel, and a similar conclusion reached. Moreover, the
number of workers employed in capital-producing industries fluctuates greatly with the cycle, but very little
in other industries.

The demand for workers at the beginning of the
period of advance is met by the absorption of the unemployed. In periods of intense prosperity additional
workers are drawn partly from the increase in population,[2] partly from agriculture. As is well known, there
has been a drift of population from agriculture to industry in all the industrial states of Europe and, we
may add, also in America.[3] The stream, however, has
not been steady. The surplus agricultural population

[1] Cassel, op. cit. p. 519.

[2] This factor had previously been developed by L. Pohle, but Cassel's
analysis is essentially different.

[3] See Spiethoff, "Krisen," *Handwörterbuch der Staatswissenschaften*
(1925), VI, pp. 75, 77.

has been kept on the land during periods of depression until it could be absorbed by the capital-producing industries in periods of advance. Without these reserves of labor, periods of prosperity could not have assumed the proportions they have hitherto attained. The migration from agriculture to industry has been due to the revolution in the whole economic organization during the last hundred years. But sooner or later a state of equilibrium between agriculture and industry will be reached. The stream from agriculture to industry will then materially diminish. Here, then, is a factor which in the future will tend to tone down extreme cyclical fluctuations.[1] "If it is clear that the capacity of agriculture to provide labor is now materially curtailed at the close of the industrial revolution, we reach the important conclusion that the *conjuncture movements are, to a very great extent, a phenomenon of the period of transition from the old economic forms to the modern.*" [2]

The business cycle, then, according to Spiethoff and Cassel, consists essentially of fluctuations in the production of fixed capital. This view is quite in accord

---

[1] Cassel, op. cit. pp. 537–544. The limiting influence of available workers calls to mind Spiethoff's theory of the failure of complementary goods (labor and the subsistence of labor) to balance the enormous output of fixed capital. This lack of proportionality disrupts the prosperity period. Cf. *Jahrbuch für Gesetzgebung*, 1903, p. 698.

[2] Cassel, op. cit. p. 545. Cassel points to the fact that cyclical fluctuations have been most violent in the United States, where an almost unlimited labor supply was available through immigration. See also Harry Jerome, *Migration and Business Cycles*.

with the statement of Foster and Catchings that we
make progress only while we are adding to our industrial equipment.[1] But now what causes these fluctuations in the production of fixed capital? In answer to
this question there have arisen two schools of thought,
which are, however, not mutually exclusive, and occa-
sionally we find the same writer (for example, Cassel)
giving some weight to each factor, while at the same
time giving special emphasis to one. One group finds
the answer in the dynamics of production; the other,
in the dynamics of consumption. But whatever the
moving causes giving the initial impulse, both schools
agree that the fluctuations follow from the reactions
of the initial forces upon a system of production which
is capitalistic, or roundabout.

A. INVENTIONS, DISCOVERIES, AND INNOVATIONS AS IMPELLING FACTORS DISTURBING THE ECONOMIC EQUILIBRIUM

The first group find the moving factors in changes
in the technique of production. New inventions; new
processes; new territories with rich natural resources,
— all these profoundly alter the technical processes,
the average rate of return derived from fixed capital, the relative demand for fixed capital compared
with consumption goods, and therefore the production
of fixed capital. Technical improvements and the
opening of new resources are the predominant impelling factors in the upward movement of the business

[1] *Profits*, pp. 409–410.

cycle. J. M. Clark speaks of the business cycle as "an unexpected by-product of changes in methods of production." [1]

We shall note particularly the significant place given to these factors by Spiethoff,[2] Schumpeter,[3] and Cassel.[4] Other writers who have emphasized these factors are Robertson [5] and Adams.[6]

According to Spiethoff prosperity is initiated when new territories or new inventions open up new opportunities for investment of fixed capital. The accumulation of idle capital during the depression produces after a while a corrective, but that alone is not sufficient. Through the pressure of the mobile loan capital its rate of interest falls continually lower, and when this tendency coincides with the recovery of the rate of profit in industry a certain condition of equilibrium may be reached. But the entrepreneurs have need for *special* inducements for great investments, and without these a large production of fixed capital will not come. If un-

[1] *American Economic Review*, Supplement, March, 1923. Pigou remarks that inventions are capable of "setting up a rhythmical effect without themselves recurring rhythmically" (*The Economics of Welfare*, p. 828). See also Pigou, *Industrial Fluctuations*, pp. 41–44.

[2] "Vorbemerkungen zu einer Theorie der Überproduktion," *Jahrbuch für Gesetzegbung*, 1902, pp. 730–733, 748–749, 754–755, 758–759; "Krisen," *Handwörterbuch der Staatswissenschaften* (1925), VI, pp. 70–74.

[3] "Die Wellenbewegung des Wirtschaftslebens," *Archiv für Sozialwissenschaft*, 1914.

[4] Op. cit. pp. 556–562, 599, 620–623.

[5] *A Study of Industrial Fluctuations* (1915), pp. 66–68.

[6] *Economics of Business Cycles* (1925), pp. 138–145, 193–197, 224–233.

usual opportunities for gain appear, an excessive production of fixed capital will probably ensue. If, on the other hand, great losses have recently been sustained, an exaggerated fear of capital investment will prevail. The production of fixed capital is therefore never uniformly progressive, but always by fits and starts, and is followed by reaction and depression. Every false estimate of the future needs, every great technical change, must disturb the equilibrium of prices and the harmony of consumption and production.[1]

If we stand at the beginning of a new time of outstanding inventions, then the end of crises is not in sight. Moreover, the territories which are to be added to the European industrial *Kultur* carry similar obstacles and dangers, for every addition of new territory carries with it the tendency to excesses and overproduction. If industry is on the forward march in its extent and spread over peoples who have not yet been made its subjects, then there is a poor outlook for the prevention of the periodic crises. But we may expect that by the progress of social reform, by a continued adaptation to the capitalistic manner of production, the industrial catastrophes will take on a more and more civilized form and finally lose themselves in a milder crossing from prosperity to depression. This development is not a necessary one, but it is worthy of our earnest labor and effort, and it is also a possible one.[2]

---

[1] Spiethoff, "Vorbemerkungen," pp. 748–749, 754–755.
[2] Ibid. pp. 758–759.

Schumpeter says that whenever an innovation is introduced into the productive or commercial process of an industry its influence spreads at once beyond the circle of those immediately affected. Suppose a cheaper raw material is discovered. Consumers gain in lower prices, and part of their purchasing power is set free and turned in other directions. The new demand brings price increases in certain fields and a consequent shifting of profits. Any innovation — be it a new method of production, new goods, the opening up of a new market, any new combination of productive forces — will alter the buying power of consumers, the prices of raw materials, the quantity of sales, etc. These are the basic facts upon which industrial plans are formed. The old plans, formerly correct, no longer fit the facts of the industrial situation. A process of accommodation to the new facts, a fitting of the innovation into the general industrial system, becomes necessary. If the innovations appear simultaneously and in large numbers, then the data change so rapidly that adjustment becomes extremely difficult. Little by little the adjustment is made and a new equilibrium is reached. We may define the period of depression as one in which there is being completed an accommodation to the new industrial situation created in the preceding period by the appearance of many relatively sudden innovations. A reorganization of the price system, of incomes, of production to fit the new demand situation,[1] is inevitable. This proc-

[1] Cf. A. A. Young, *American Economic Review*, Supplement, 1923, p. 11.

ess is the content of the period of depression, and it takes place with losses, resistance, and disillusionment. Thus we come to the conclusion that it is the multiplicity of innovations in the period of prosperity which disturbs the equilibrium and changes the basic industrial data so that a period of readjustment of prices, values, and production necessarily appears.[1]

But why do these innovations appear in mass? We must here distinguish between innovation *possibilities* and the *practical realization* of these possibilities. Prosperity does not arise merely as a result of discoveries. It waits upon the actual development of these innovations. It waits upon the appearance of "undertaker activity,"[2] which is the driving power of the period of prosperity. Only a very small part of the business population has the intelligence and the energy to found new undertakings, to develop successfully new possibilities. But while only a very few can take the *lead*, many can *follow*. Once someone has gone ahead, it is not so difficult to imitate him. Few are capable of securing financial backing for a new venture of which bankers and investors are skeptical; but once one such establishment is a going concern, others can easily secure credit and capital for similar undertakings.[3] If a new

[1] Schumpeter, "Die Wellenbewegung des Wirtschaftslebens," *Archiv für Sozialwissenschaft*, pp. 17–20, 23–24.

[2] See also M. T. England, "Analysis of the Crises Cycle," *Journal of Political Economy*, October, 1913, pp. 712–734.

[3] See also Spiethoff, "Krisen," *Handwörterbuch der Staatswissenschaften* (1925), VI, pp. 70–71.

process is put into successful operation, others can simply copy. If the first one has found the right location, others can locate near him. Experiments with workers and customers benefit those who follow. Even so, the problems facing those who imitate innovators are more difficult than those of the ordinary routine business. But they are not nearly so great as those faced by the leaders who blaze the trail. Thus, whenever a few successful innovators appear, immediately a host of others follow them. This is the basis of the "wave movement" of the industrial life.[1]

Cassel holds that a "conjuncture-movement" which has become much enfeebled — run down, so to speak — is bound to be restored to full strength by some new technical advance. Moreover, the opening up of new countries creates a new demand for fixed capital — transport, bridges, houses, etc. This source of the revival of prosperity will eventually disappear, but there are still great tasks for the world economy to face before the whole world is more or less completely equipped with the material foundations of European civilization. Every new opportunity to use fixed capital profitably on a large scale acts as a cause of a new "high conjuncture." The man who complains of business cycles and condemns the social order that facilitates or permits them is really complaining of the advance of our material civilization. The fluctuating movement of the business cycle is an outcome of the struggles of the

[1] Schumpeter, op. cit. pp. 28–32.

social will to progress; and as long as the material conditions of the satisfaction of this desire require a large use of fixed capital, we must expect fluctuations in the productive activity of the community akin to the present business-cycle movement.[1]

But how do these factors work themselves out? Here we are forced to consider the effect of these technical changes on the prospective earnings of fixed capital, the resulting effect on the distribution of a nation's income over time — in a word, the effect on the rate of interest and the shifts in the utilization of the nation's income in the purchase of fixed capital compared with the purchase of consumers' goods. In this analysis the writers that we shall consider are Fisher, Wicksell, Cassel, Halm, Röpke, Robertson, Pigou, and Spiethoff.

New inventions, new processes, and new resources increase the productivity of fixed capital and so raise the rate of interest. When inventions or scientific and geographical discoveries are made, the effect is to reduce the immediate income stream of the community for the

[1] Cassel, op. cit. pp. 620–623. So also Taussig speaks of the effect of rapid changes in the arts: "Crises have appeared in the largest scale and with the widest effects during the period since the Industrial Revolution and in the countries whose progress has been most rapid" (*Principles of Economics* (1921), Vol. I, p. 391). Note also the following from W. H. Beveridge: "If the whole of the national dividend each year were devoted to immediate consumption and none to multiplying the means of production, if, in fact, there were no saving, there would be no possibility of industrial growth, and therefore no possibility of the dislocations incident to that growth" (*Unemployment*, p. 62).

sake of increasing the remoter income stream, and therefore to increase the rate of time preference and the rate of interest.

The inventions of Watt and others, which led to the present railway system, are cases in point. They caused the income-stream of society, from being fairly uniform, to assume a rapidly ascending form. . . . Throughout the period of railway building, social income has been a series of investment, return, and partial re-investment, and a curve which would depict the actual income enjoyed would show it to be sharply ascending Numerous other inventions have co-operated to this end A whole series of new appliances have followed the discovery of electricity. The elevator and the steel skeleton have revolutionized building.[1]

The net effect of inventions and discoveries, then, is to increase the investment in fixed capital.

Society, instead of confining its productive energies to the old channels and obtaining a relatively immediate return in enjoyable income, as by producing food products, clothing, etc., directs its labor to great engineering enterprises such as constructing tunnels, subways, waterworks, and irrigation systems, that is, to instruments which cannot begin to contribute a return in enjoyable income for many years.[2]

Inventions and improvements raise the average rate of profit and the productivity of real capital. But the

[1] Irving Fisher, *The Rate of Interest*, pp. 200–201. The Macmillan Company.
[2] Ibid. p. 203.

current market rate of interest or discount is not raised at once; and when it is, the rise is not (for a time, at least) as great as the increase in the average rate of profit. There are several reasons for this. In the first place, at the beginning of revival, banks have a considerable volume of lending power at their disposal, and they are not likely to raise the discount rates immediately until their reserves are beginning to be more or less seriously encroached upon, for somewhat the same reason that wages do not rise until the "industrial reserve army" is beginning to be depleted by the increasing demand for labor.[1] Moreover, as Fisher has pointed out, borrowers are likely to have more foresight than lenders. Borrowers are more likely to be awake to the possibilities of profit-making inherent in the new inventions and discoveries; hence, while the borrower is willing to pay a higher interest for the loan than before, lenders are willing to lend for the same interest. This disparity has the effect that the market rate of interest will not rise as high as if both sides saw the conditions equally well.[2]

With high prospective profits and relatively low rates of interest on the loan market the tendency will be for entrepreneurs to buy or construct fixed capital in large quantities. The result is a rise in prices, as Knut Wicksell has pointed out. In his paper on "The Influence of the Rate of Interest on Prices"[3] he states his

---

[1] Compare with Cassel, op. cit. p. 617.

[2] Fisher, *The Rate of Interest*, pp. 285–286.

[3] *Economic Journal*, June, 1907, pp. 213, 215.

thesis as follows: If the leading banks of the world were to lower their rate of interest, say 1 per cent below its ordinary level, and keep it so for some years, then the prices of all commodities would rise and rise without any limit whatever; if they were to raise the rate of interest 1 per cent above its normal level, and keep it so for some years, then all prices would fall and fall without any limit except zero. When the market rate of interest diverges from the profit rate, the effect is a change in prices. The price level is the connecting link between the interest rate and the profit rate.[1] Wicksell's statement assumes an arbitrary lowering or raising of the interest rate by the artificial control of the banks. But, of course, the same effect would follow if through inventions or improvements the rate of profit were raised temporarily above the market rate of interest.

If building companies and railway companies are able to raise money at 4 per cent instead of 5 per cent, they can offer, and by competition will be compelled to offer, for wages and materials, anything up to 25 per cent *more* than before (4 per cent on $125 being the same as 5 per cent on $100). Thus prices rise, and they will continue to rise so long as the rate of interest lags behind its

[1] "A lowering of the interest rate means an increase in the buying power of the entrepreneurial class, therewith a growing demand for real capital and an increase in the prices of these goods. ... If the money interest is lowered, then that means a sharpening of the competition on the part of the undertakers with reference to the real capital. The prices of the means of production have now a tendency to rise."—Wilhelm Röpke, "Kredit und Konjunktur," *Jahrbücher für Nationalökonomie und Statistik*, 1926, pp. 270, 272

normal rate ; that is, the rate consistent with the existing marginal productivity of real capital.[1]

The opposite of all this will take place when the rate of
interest has become too high in proportion to average
profit, and so in both cases a difference between the two
rates remaining, the movement of prices can never cease,
just as the electric current never ceases as long as the
difference of tension between the poles remains.[2]

Whenever, then, inventions, improvements, and new
resources raise the prospective rate of profit above the
market rate on loans, an impelling force is released
which leads to an expansion in the production of fixed
capital. The "inequality of foresight" which keeps the
loan market rate below the prospective profit rate
"produces overinvestment during rising prices and
relative stagnation during falling prices. In the former case society is trapped into devoting too much
investment of productive energies for future return,
while in the contrary case, underinvestment is the
rule."[3]

A discrepancy of one or two points between the rate
of interest as it is and as it should be is therefore of
no trifling importance. Its cumulative effects, although
seldom realized, are serious. ... The truth is that the
rate of interest is not a narrow phenomenon applying only
to a few business contracts, but permeates all economic

[1] Wicksell, op. cit. p. 216.
[2] Wicksell, in the *Economic Journal*, June, 1907, p. 216.
[3] Fisher, *The Rate of Interest*, pp. 286–287.

relations. It is the link which binds man to the future and by which he makes all his far-reaching decisions.[1]

Cassel comes to a similar conclusion. Of all the "impelling forces" that affect the production of fixed capital the interest rate occupies the central place.[2]

Inventions, improvements, and new resources thus bring about an increase in the production of fixed capital and, incidentally, a rise in the level of prices. This rise in prices has a profound influence upon the distribution of the community's income, upon the income directed toward consumption, and upon the volume of savings. Several writers[3] have recently pointed out that the activity which we call saving is carried on under two conditions: (1) voluntary and (2) compulsory.

[1] Ibid. p. 336. See also Röpke, op. cit., particularly the following: "The absolute height or the absolute change of the interest rate is not decisive for the effects of the interest oscillations on the price level, but, as we have seen, the difference between the money interest and the real interest. If the money interest is higher than the real interest, then the price level has a tendency to sink; if it is lower than the real interest, then the price level has a tendency to rise" (p. 274).

[2] Cassel, op. cit. p. 614. See also A. A. Young, *American Economic Review*, Supplement, 1923, pp. 8–10.

[3] Cf. A. C. Pigou, in *Is Unemployment Inevitable?* (pp. 100–111); D. H. Robertson, *Banking Policy and the Price Level* (1926); Georg Halm, "Das Zinsproblem am Geld- und Kapitalmarkt," *Jahrbücher für Nationalökonomie und Statistik*, July and August, 1926; Wilhelm Röpke, "Kredit und Konjunktur," *Jahrbücher für Nationalökonomie und Statistik*, March–April, 1926; Alvin H. Hansen, *Cycles of Prosperity and Depression* (1921), pp. 104–106; "Factors affecting the Trend of Real Wages," *American Economic Review*, March, 1925, p. 40; Albert Hahn, *Geld und Kredit* (1924); B. M. Anderson, "Bank Money and the Capital Supply," *The Chase Economic Bulletin*, Vol. VI, No. 3; J. Schumpeter, *Theorie der wirtschaftlichen Entwicklung* (1926).

Attention should first be called to the elementary and well-known fact that there are two kinds of real capital: (1) fixed capital and (2) circulating capital. The former includes equipment and plant; the latter is described by Robertson as "shifting congeries of goods in all stages of production from the soil to the consumer." The value of circulating capital bears a relation to the value of the total annual output of goods which depends upon the length of the average period of production.[1] Moreover, if the process of production is absolutely uniform throughout the period of production the value of circulating capital at any moment is equal to half the value of the goods produced during a production period, which production period may be several years long, the exact length depending upon the degree of "round-aboutness" of the process.

Now the "capital disposal" — to use Cassel's phrase — which is invested in fixed capital is usually (but not always) obtained from the capital market. The capital disposal which is supplied on the capital market consists of savings made by individuals and corporations from current income. As Cassel puts it: "On the capital market the savings appear as supply, while the real capital produced appears as demand for the disposal of capital." [2] On the other hand, a considerable part of

[1] Cf. E. V. Böhm-Bawerk, *Positive Theory of Capital* (Stechert reprint), pp. 403–424.

[2] Cassel, *A Theory of Social Economy*, p. 597. See also Spiethoff, "Krisen," *Handwörterbuch der Staatswissenschaften* (1925), Vol. VI, p. 76.

the supply of capital disposal required in the production and holding of circulating capital is supplied by the money market, by bank loans. A part is supplied out of profits, and a part from the capital market by means of long-time loans.[1] The saving required for the production and storing of circulating capital is released by the sale of the stocks, and made available for reinvestment in a further batch of goods. When finally the raw materials and semifinished products have been worked up into finished fixed-capital goods and are sold to the manufacturer, or when the lumber, mortar, brick, stone, or other materials have finally gone into the building of a factory or house, the short-time capital disposal which carried it during the production stage must now be converted into long-time capital disposal. Thus the goods pass from the money market over to the capital market. "In the place of the producer or his loan giver steps the buyer of the real capital or his loan giver."[2] The

---

[1] R. G. Hawtrey, "Mr. Robertson on Banking Policy," *Economic Journal*, September, 1926. Note especially the following: "In practice a very large part of the total amount of circulating capital is provided by way of *permanent* investment in the form of share capital, debentures, or partnership capital. There is no reason why a trader should procure the whole of his working capital by means of bank advances. It is more usual for him to cover from his permanent capital not only all his fixed plant, but the minimum to which his working capital is likely to sink. Bank advances need only provide for the margin between the actual working capital at any time and the minimum. The purpose of so providing for this fluctuating margin is to avoid having to accumulate a balance of idle money at any time when the working capital in use is small."

[2] Halm, op. cit. p. 14. Compare with Robertson, op. cit. p. 85.

capital disposal necessary for production is thus set free and can again be used for further production, while the capital disposal of the capital market steps in and takes over the fixed capital and remains incorporated in it until it is worn out.[1]

While fixed capital is in process of being produced it assumes the form of circulating capital. Only when the material of which it is constructed is finally finished into buildings, machinery, etc. does it become fixed capital. The *process of producing* fixed capital thus implies an increase in circulating capital, and this increase in circulating capital is financed in a large part by capital disposal furnished by the banks.[2] Because this capital

---

[1] "Thus an increase in the rate of output of instruments from, say, 100 units to 120 units per production period requires, if equilibrium is to be preserved, not only a single permanent increase of between 10 and 20 units of Short Lacking [short-time saving], but an additional supply, *in every succeeding production-period*, of 20 units of Long Lacking [long-time saving]." — D. H. Robertson, *Banking Policy and the Price Level* (P. S. King & Son), p. 85

[2] Part of it is furnished by entrepreneurs. But even this action is likely to affect the general public. Thus Pigou says: "When business men, moved by optimism, decide to spend a larger proportion of their balances in hiring workmen to make for them manufactured goods and industrial equipment, what they do, in effect, is to give to shopkeepers more of their money in return for goods of the kind on which workpeople spend their wages. In consequence, shopkeepers put up the prices of these goods and sell rather less of them to persons in receipt of fixed incomes, and also, in spite of this, for the time being find their own stocks of them somewhat reduced. The business community has thus secured the extra stuff that it needs for paying wages partly by depleting shopkeepers' stocks and partly by forcing the owners of fixed incomes to content themselves with smaller purchases" (in *Is Unemployment Inevitable?* (Macmillan & Company, Limited), pp. 99–100).

disposal is furnished by the issue of bank credit, it has sometimes been supposed that we here encounter an exception to the classic doctrine that all capital is saved.[1] But the case is not so simple. You cannot get something for nothing. You cannot create real capital out of thin air. You cannot increase the real income of a nation merely by increasing its money income. The real purchasing power is not greater, even though the nominal purchasing power is increased. The capital disposal furnished by the banks represents compulsory

[1] Thus H. G. Moulton says that "an expanding bank currency during periods of business recovery will provide the funds for new capital formation without a curtailment of consumption" ("Commercial Banking and Capital Formation," *Journal of Political Economy*, November, 1918, p. 878). In so far as the expansion of bank currency is accompanied by an immediate increase in the production and market supply of consumers' goods this statement is true so far as the total national consumption is concerned. But it is not true of large classes of consumers, nor is it true relative to the total real income of the community. The reverse of Moulton's position is well stated by D. H. Robertson in his *Banking Policy and the Price Level*, pp. 54–55. Let us suppose, he says, an increase in individual productivity. "If the banks take no action there will be a fall in the price-level and an increase in the real value of the public's money stocks. . . . By making additional loans of an appropriate amount at an appropriate pace, the bank can counteract the fall in the price-level, and, without occasioning a rise, can extract from the public an amount of Lacking [saving] . . . equal to the increase which would otherwise have automatically taken place in the real value of the public's money stocks." Thus, owing to the "increase in productivity the bank has been able, without causing a rise in the price-level, to impose upon the public a quantity of Lacking whose imposition would have necessitated a rise in the price-level if there had been no increase in productivity." On the other hand, suppose the individual productivity constant, but that there is an increase in total output due to the absorption into employment of an increment of population. During "the produc-

saving.[1] Every issue of bank credit reduces the value of the "unspent margin," to use Hawtrey's phrase. When banks issue new credit to business men, these business men in turn use the proceeds for two purposes: (1) to enlarge their stocks of raw materials or semi-finished or finished products; (2) to increase their output in the various stages of the productive process. These funds are therefore passed on to wage-earners and firms supplying materials, whether raw or semifinished. The latter in turn use the funds to increase their stocks and enlarge their output, and in part, perhaps, to increase their own consumption (through taking a larger

tion period when Circulating Capital is being increased but output is still unaffected, Imposed Lacking is inflicted on the public, and a price-level higher than that prevailing at the beginning of the period is established."

Mr. Moulton tells us that in the half century from 1866 to 1916 the loans and investments of commercial banks increased nearly twenty-four billions of dollars, and that this gradually expanding volume of bank currency "has made it possible for business men to secure the funds with which to induce human energy to create capital goods without antecedent saving on the part of consumers. As a result of this process of expanding the volume of loanable funds, we find that a smaller curtailment of consumption is required in order to release funds for capital formation" (op. cit. p. 869). To this Mr. Robertson would no doubt reply that had it not been for this expansion of bank credit the price level would have fallen, which fall would have increased the value of the public's money incomes. The expansion of bank credit prevented this fall in prices, and so robbed the public of the increased value of their money. Thus he would say that the twenty-four billions of dollars of capital came out of enforced saving.

[1] "The issuance of bank credit simply redistributes purchasing power, reducing the real purchasing power of income receivers generally, and increasing the purchasing power of entrepreneurs able to secure bank credit." — Alvin H. Hansen, *Cycles of Prosperity and Depression* (1921), p. 106

part of the profits for personal consumption, in a proprietorship business, or declaring larger dividends, in the case of the corporation). Thus wage-earners in particular (and stockholders and proprietors to some extent) come on the market with larger money incomes to spend. The goods offered in the market increase with the increased output but not in proportion to the increased output. The difference appears in the form of increased stocks held by dealers, wholesalers, manufacturers, and raw-material producers. These stocks in part consist of consumers' goods in the various stages on the march to the consumer and in part of unfinished capital goods. But they are all on the march to the final purchaser (whether consumer or producer), and in their present stage are, properly speaking, circulating capital. The new buying power (consequent upon the issue of bank credit) implies a "renunciation on the part of the possessors of the old buying power, who, as it were, must move closer together like the passengers in a railroad compartment when there enters a new passenger."[1] This amounts to an enforced retrenchment of consumption[2] on the part of the possessors of the old buying power, and this compulsory saving is the

[1] Cf. Röpke, op. cit. p. 250.

[2] Pigou says what "happens is exactly the same as what would happen if, the general level of prices being kept constant, a tax were imposed on the owners of fixed money incomes and the proceeds handed over as a sort of bounty to the business community" (*Is Unemployment Inevitable?* p. 100). See also Hahn, *Geld und Kredit*, pp. 58–59.

source of the capital disposal invested in the stocks of circulating capital which have been produced.[1]

Eventually a portion of the stock of circulating capital will appear as finished fixed-capital goods. These goods must now be taken over from the short-time capital disposal market by the long-time capital disposal market. In short, they must find permanent investors. These investors furnish the necessary purchasing power out of savings from their incomes, thus deflecting their purchasing power from consumption to accumulation. The latter method of providing capital disposal does not necessitate a rise in the price level, whereas the bank-credit method of providing capital disposal involves compulsory saving squeezed out of income-receivers through a rise in prices. The banking system can only provide capital disposal or savings "by extorting it from the general public through the multiplication of currency."[2]

We note, then, that the expansion of production is not ordinarily financed out of voluntary savings. The increased money incomes are, in the first instance, in large part directed toward consumers' goods; but the wills of the consumers are thwarted by the increase in price, forcing them against their wishes and designs to

[1] See also the article by the present writer in the *American Economic Review*, March, 1925, p. 40. "The capital equipment came immediately out of the savings of the corporations, but ultimately and in reality out of the enforced saving imposed, by the rise in the price level, upon wage-earners, salaried people, bond and mortgage holders, insurance-policy holders, etc."

[2] Cf. Robertson, op. cit. p. 89.

furnish the capital disposal needed to carry the increased stocks of circulating capital.[1]

Through the bank credit there is opened up to the enterprisers access to the general industrial stream of goods before they have secured the normal claim upon it. . . . The maintenance of credit, in a sense, operates like a command to industry to yield itself to the purposes of the enterpriser, and serves to give him a check on the goods which he needs and to turn over to him the control over the productive forces. Only in this way can the industrial development be accomplished . . . , and this is the fundamental function of the modern credit structure.[2]

Thus the expansion of production of fixed capital consequent upon new technical innovations results in "deep-gripping changes" in the general industrial situation "which can all be brought under the formula variations in the relations between accumulation and consumption."[3] There is a shifting of the national production in the direction of a relatively greater production of fixed capital. The total income of a certain

[1] It may well be that certain groups enjoy a larger real income in spite of the enforced saving. Thus wage-earners regularly find their wage rates reduced in rising-price periods, yet their annual earnings are larger because of the increased employment. But that does not obviate the fact that they are none the less taxed by the rise in prices, as is shown by the reduction of their real wage rates. They get less pay for the work done, but they get larger real incomes by doing more work. Other groups are less fortunate. Salaried people, bond and mortgage holders, insurance-policy holders, suffer a dead loss due to the decline in the purchasing power of their fixed money incomes.

[2] Röpke, op. cit. p. 254.

[3] Ibid. p. 264.

period is just sufficient to purchase the production of that period. But the income is divided into what is consumed and what is saved. The first part goes to purchase consumables; the second part goes to purchase the newly produced real capital. The expansion of bank credit means a diversion of the community's purchasing power in the direction of capital goods. This implies a corresponding diversion of production, the supply of consumers' goods being *relatively* cut down. "Thus the action of the banks has the same effect as an increase of the savings of the community upon the distribution of the collective purchasing power between capital goods and consumers' goods." [1] In the opening of the period of advance there is a "change in the disposal of income in the direction of increased saving. This raises purchasing power as regards capital goods, and generally to a greater extent than the production of such goods. Hence in this period we must expect a general rise in the prices of fixed capital." [2]

Toward the close of prosperity profits fall, because of the advance of cost prices (notably wages and the prices of raw materials), and so voluntary saving tends to decline.[3] But the production of fixed capital maintains its

[1] Cassel, *Theory of Social Economy*, p. 600.

[2] Ibid. pp. 598–599.

[3] "This is all the more likely since towards the end of a boom the resources of important classes of investors have been trenched upon by rising real costs of production and by a reversal of the tendency, which marks the early stages of the expansion, for profits to encroach upon wages" (Robertson, *Banking Policy and the Price Level*, p. 88). Cf. also Mitchell, *Business Cycles*, chap. xi, and Lescure, op. cit. p. 386.

upward movement and sometimes even increases it. There is thus a change in the disposal of income opposite to that in the sphere of production. A stringency develops on the capital market, and the prices of capital goods fall.[1] It is possible "that at this stage the producers of instruments, rather than restrict the scale of their output, should be willing to charge themselves with the responsibility for procuring not merely the Short Lacking required to carry these instruments during their period of gestation, but the Long Lacking required to carry them for some time after their birth. From both these sources a call is made on the banking system to 'provide' those increased supplies of Long Lacking for which reliance can no longer be placed on investors. Now the banking system can, of course, only 'provide' Long Lacking in the same way that it 'provides' Short Lacking, namely, by extorting it from the general public through the multiplication of currency."[2]

Robertson, moreover, points out the complementary nature of long-time capital disposal and short-time capital disposal. Not only do instruments require short-time capital disposal while they are being constructed, but also after they are finished, for their *operation*.

Towards the end of a constructional boom, therefore, the pressure on the banking system is increased, and the rise in general prices aggravated, by the demands of the owners of numerous new instruments for Short Lacking to enable them to keep the instruments in operation.[3]

[1] Cassel, op. cit. p. 599.   [2] Robertson, op. cit. pp. 88–89.   [3] Ibid. p. 92.

In Cassel's view a crisis "*does not mean overproduction or an overestimate of the demands of consumers or the needs of the community for the services of fixed capital, but an overestimate of the supply of capital, or of the amount of savings available for taking over the real capital produced.* What is overestimated is the capacity of the capitalists to provide savings in sufficient quantity." [1] This capacity has to be estimated several years in advance. "It is, therefore, quite possible that enterprises, such as the construction of houses, railways, etc., will be planned, and even begun, in such quantities that, when their need of capital afterwards makes itself felt, it cannot be satisfied." [2]

"That the crisis really consists in an acute scarcity of capital — that is to say, of savings — to purchase the real capital produced is partly shown by the great difficulty of selling the ready-made fixed capital or getting means to pay the costs of its production, and partly by the very general inability to complete undertakings that have been begun." [3] This difficulty naturally reacts upon the production of fixed capital. This restriction first hits the building trades. Hence the strain of the capital market leads to a decline of building operations. But the construction of railways, tramways, canals, electrical works, etc. require more time. In spite of the strain in the capital market they must be completed if

[1] Cassel, op. cit. pp. 625–626.
[2] Ibid. p. 626; see also Mitchell, *Business Cycles*, p. 560.
[3] Cassel, op. cit. p. 628.

possible.[1] Hence the production of fixed capital and materials continues to rise in spite of the difficulty of getting capital.[2]

If sufficient capital disposal cannot be obtained through saving, then business men will turn to the banks for funds.[3] Because of this encroachment of the investment market upon the money market, there arises a great shortage of short-time capital disposal. This makes it difficult if not impossible to secure adequate working capital.[4]

Several writers have emphasized the obstacles encountered in the last phase of prosperity arising from the

[1] Aftalion (*Les Crises périodiques de surproduction*, 1913) presents statistics to show that the horse power in various industries continues to increase from one to three years after the break in prices.

[2] Ibid. pp. 610–611. Other writers who lay stress on the scarcity of capital disposal toward the end of the prosperity period are Tougan-Baranowsky, Spiethoff, Taussig, and Mitchell. From Spiethoff we have the following: "But the capital-producing industries suffer toward the end of a period of prosperity from a shortage of capital seeking investment" ("Vorbemerkungen," op. cit. p. 725). He frequently speaks of production having gone beyond the "available investment-seeking capital" (cf. pp. 731–732, 737, 744, 751). See also Mitchell, *Business Cycles*, pp. 573–574. From Taussig we have the following: "New enterprises now find it difficult to get support; while those already launched find it harder and harder to procure the additional funds needed for completing their outfit. . . . There is likely to be maladjustment in a greater addition to the total of the community's capital than is justified by the total of its available savings" (*Principles of Economics* (3d ed.) Vol. I, pp. 399–400).

[3] Halm, in his article on "Das Zinsproblem am Geld- und Kapitalmarkt" (*Jahrbücher für Nationalökonomie und Statistik*, July, 1926), speaks of "the elastic money market" as taking over the task of supplying capital disposal for the "burdened capital market" (p. 15).

[4] Ibid. pp. 27–34.

scarcity of labor and of raw materials. We have already noted that Cassel emphasizes the scarcity of labor as a limiting factor; so, also, Spiethoff.[1] Sombart emphasizes the limitations of organic raw materials.[2] Allyn Young points out that the supply of labor and raw materials is elastic only within limits.[3] In short, a disproportionality develops between the fixed and auxiliary factors of production. That too much fixed capital of particular types can be produced is obvious from the law of proportionality of factors. If too much fixed capital has been produced relative to the available supply of auxiliary factors, then you have unused capacity, social waste, and financial loss, all of which necessitate a readjustment before a true economic equilibrium is reached. The quantity of fixed capital that can economically be utilized in a certain technical process has relatively fixed limits due to the limitation of auxiliary factors, notably labor and certain raw materials. Why, then, is too much fixed capital produced? The answer is that the production of fixed capital takes place in anticipation of *future* demand, and this is impossible to forecast accurately, especially in a competitive society where each producer is unaware of the amount of fixed

[1] Spiethoff, *Jahrbuch für Gesetzgebung*, 1903, p. 698. See also Spiethoff's article on "Krisen" in the *Handwörterbuch der Staatswissenschaften* (1925), VI, p. 77.

[2] Cf. Mitchell, *Business Cycles*, p. 16; Werner Sombart, *Hochkapitalismus* (1927), pp. 577–582.

[3] "The Trend of Prices," *American Economic Review*, Supplement, March, 1923, p. 10.

capital which his competitors are constructing. This forecast is rendered all the more difficult because of the length of time required to produce fixed capital. A long time must elapse before the forecasts are brought to the acid test of the facts — facts relating not only to the volume of consumer demand, but more especially relating to the best possible combination of factors, or the proper proportion of fixed capital in relation to the available supply of auxiliary factors. At the end of the production period it may be discovered that a disproportionate quantity of fixed capital [1] is available in view of the limited supply of auxiliary factors.

Say, Ricardo, and Mill were quite right in their insistence that overproduction is inconceivable. Industry is continually engaged in a struggle to ward off scarcity of goods in proportion to human needs. "In the battle against need there can on the whole never be too many troops, but they may be massed in one place, which means too few in another." [2] It is quite possible that the *relative* supply of the different factors of production is not properly proportioned. Thus Röpke rightly says that "the stronger and more sudden the enlargement of the general accumulation, the more does the fungus of

[1] It should be noted that even though the overbuilt fixed capital yielded a zero return on the fixed investment this does not imply a zero interest rate. For the interest rate is not fixed by past earnings, but by prospective earnings of funds currently available in the loan markets and by the consumption demand for loans (time preference of consumers). Past investments may earn no interest, but current funds still will.

[2] Röpke, op. cit. p. 259.

disproportionality nest itself in the general economic system. ... Every crisis is a certificate to this fact that we would have let the trees of accumulation grow unto heaven. The stronger we attempt to widen the boundaries of the accumulation increase, so much stronger is the recoil." [1]

According to this group of writers, then, the main factor that brings prosperity to a close is the failure of an adequate supply of capital disposal. This scarcity reveals itself in a high interest rate and the fall in the price of fixed capital goods, and is aggravated by the rise of prime costs — the high prices paid for labor and materials toward the close of the period of prosperity. The difficulty arises from a disproportionality between the disposal of the community's income and the disposal

[1] Röpke, op. cit. p. 260. Robertson and Spiethoff, moreover, both speak of a lack of proportionality between the production of fixed capital and consumable goods. This from Robertson: "To a large extent ... fluctuations in the desirability of acquiring instruments are the inevitable penalty of industrial progress; but they are also to a certain limited extent attributable to an avoidable lack of responsiveness in the flow of consumable goods required to co-operate with those instruments in the form of real wages." Consumable goods are "the constituents of real wages" (*Banking Policy and the Price Level*, pp. 94–96). From Spiethoff, the following: "A part of the capital goods cannot, therefore, be turned to profitable account, since alone they do not reach that far, but need to be supplemented by laborers and their means of subsistence." These latter are the supplementary goods which are scarce in comparison with the relatively overproduced capital goods ("Krisen," *Handwörterbuch* (1925), VI, p. 78). It is not evident, however, that there is any shortage of finished goods *in stock*; and if there were, as Hawtrey points out, far from damping down production such shortage would directly stimulate it (*Economic Journal*, September, 1926).

of its productive forces. There arises, moreover, a disproportionality between the fixed capital and its cooperant factors of production — labor, raw materials,[1] and the goods which labor consumes. This shows itself in the disproportionate rise of wages, prices of raw materials, and cost of living toward the close of the period of prosperity.

With these writers, then, the *impelling* forces are inventions, discoveries, new resources, innovations in technical processes or products, which increase the prospective rate of profit, arouse the spirit of enterprise, and stimulate the production of fixed capital. This upsets the economic equilibrium, the normal disposal of the community's income, as well as the disposal of its productive forces. The industrial community is brought back toward equilibrium by the limiting or restraining forces which operate through the price-building process. The rate of interest, the prices of labor and materials — these are the regulators of the processes of production.[2]

Why do they not act quickly enough to prevent any serious disturbance of the equilibrium? Cassel's answer is that it takes a certain amount of time for the reactions to make themselves felt. This is due to the fact that when the money rate and the real rate of interest are dislocated with respect to each other a reaction is set up

[1] Sombart emphasizes particularly the scarcity of *organic* raw materials. See summary of Sombart's views given in Mitchell's *Business Cycles*, p. 16; see also Werner Sombart, *Hochkapitalismus* (1927), pp. 577–582.

[2] Cassel, op. cit. pp. 614–617.

working through a change in the price level, which change works cumulatively to set up a further discrepancy, or lag, between the money rate and the interest rate. Eventually the cumulative reaction is checked because of the ensuing disturbances upon the disposal of income and the disposal of the productive forces.[1] The production of fixed capital requires time. The restrictive forces do not come into full force until the fixed capital is finished, until long-time capital disposal is needed to carry the fixed capital. Thus, says Cassel, the length of the conjuncture period is to some extent connected with the length of the period of production of fixed capital.[2]

Cassel asks also the question, Why is it that these restrictive reactions do not bring about a gradual balancing of the upward and downward movements, thus establishing eventually a perfect equilibrium? His answer is that they would were it not for the fact that fresh disturbing factors — new innovations in industry — are constantly throwing the equilibrium out of line.[3]

B. FLUCTUATIONS IN CONSUMER DEMAND AS IMPELLING FACTOR DISTURBING ECONOMIC EQUILIBRIUM

The capitalistic, or roundabout, system of production may be upset from a balanced equilibrium by technical innovations — new inventions, new scientific discoveries, or new natural resources. But there are other

---

[1] Cassel, op. cit. pp. 618–619.   [2] Ibid. pp. 618–619.
[3] Ibid. pp. 620–623.

dynamic factors that from time to time disturb the balance. Among the most dynamic forces in economic life are the continued fluctuations and shifts in the demands of consumers. People love variety, change, new fashions, new products, novelties of every description. The ensuing changes and shifts in demand are bound to set up disturbing reactions which upset the economic equilibrium.

In a capitalistic society which carries on production by the roundabout process very slight fluctuations in consumer demand give rise to pronounced industrial fluctuations. The leading sponsor of this view is Albert Aftalion, who wrote his "La Réalité des surproductions générales" in 1909 and expanded this work into his *Les Crises périodiques de surproduction* in 1913.

Aftalion speaks of the persistent difficulty of maintaining economic equilibrium. Observation reveals perpetual oscillations rather than a state of equilibrium. These oscillations are brought about in a régime of capitalistic production — not a juridical régime, but a technical régime making a large use of fixed capital. Once the equilibrium is broken in a capitalistic régime, the alternating series of prosperity and depression will succeed each other, and the economic organism will discover itself caught in a chain, without end, of action and reaction which constitutes the periodic cycles.[1]

[1] Aftalion, "La Réalité des surproductions générales," *Revue d'économie politique*, 1909, pp. 202–203. It will be noted that Aftalion — unlike Spiethoff, Cassel, Schumpeter, Adams, and others — believes that the cycle, once started, is self-generating.

It is the capitalistic, time-consuming process of production that transforms the small oscillations of market price around normal price, the small oscillations around the state of equilibrium, into pronounced periods of prosperity and depression. Instead of applying labor and land directly to satisfy wants, the characteristic technique of capitalism is to produce first a long series of capital goods the construction of which requires many months or even years, and by means of these, eventually, to make consumers' goods. This phase of capitalistic production, the period in which capital goods are being created, is the period of prosperity. This phase springs out of an existing scarcity of consumers' goods. This scarcity would at once be satisfied, and equilibrium restored, were it not for the fact that a long time must elapse before the completion of capital goods makes possible the increase in the output of consumers' goods.[1] It is the capitalistic technique of production which renders inevitable the prolonged disruption of economic equilibrium.

But when the capital is created, there arrives the second phase of capitalistic production in the creation of consumption goods. This is the period of depression.

[1] Bouniatian objects to this argument. He points out that the increased demand for consumption goods calls forth a more intensive use of existing equipment. Hence the revival leads at once to an increased output of consumption goods. Cf. M. Bouniatian, "Ma Théorie des crises et les critiques de M. Aftalion," *Révue d'économie politique*, 1924, pp. 659–660. It may be answered, however, that Aftalion is thinking in relative, not absolute, terms.

Its persistence over a considerable period of time follows from the long period during which fixed capital is able to function. The superabundance of goods manifests itself in a crisis.[1] The excessive production of these goods continues as long as there is an excess of the capital previously created, which, because of its great value and hence the preponderant importance of supplementary costs, it is not possible to leave unemployed. Finally, a considerable part of this fixed capital is worn out, and so there emerges a new scarcity of consumers' goods.

Aftalion does not pretend to find an exact correlation between these two stages in the process of production and the duration of the two periods of the economic cycle. The duration of production varies with each type of commodity. He contends that it is sufficient for his theory if you grant that, looking at the general economic organism, a time comes in the capitalistic production when a scarcity of goods reveals itself; later a moment when, thanks to the production of the required capital, the need begins largely to be satisfied; and finally a moment arrives when, thanks to the wearing out of a part of the capital, the glut of goods disappears. Taking industry as a whole into con-

[1] An increased supply of goods brings a decline in their marginal utilities, which expresses itself in a fall in prices. If we suppose the value of money constant, a fall in prices can arise only from a fall in the use value of goods (Aftalion, op. cit. p. 94). What Aftalion means to say is that the marginal utility of money is more constant between boom and depression than that of goods (cf. Robertson, in *Economic Journal*, 1914).

sideration, prosperity does not terminate when a single
category of capital goods is created. Not until a great
quantity of capital in the majority of industries is set
to work turning out consumers' goods does the period
of prosperity end. Likewise the period of depression
does not last until *all* the capital is used up. Prosperity and depression are not characterized by the peak
and bottom *of all prices*, but by the peak and bottom
of *most* prices. We are concerned with the general
tendency.

The capitalistic lengthening of the process of production is, then, in Aftalion's view, the factor which determines the amplitude of the oscillations around the
equilibrium and the duration of prosperity and depression. Nothing more, he thinks, is needed to explain the
periodicity of the cycle or the emergence of crises from
prosperity, and prosperity from depression. The longer
the process of production, the longer is the duration of
prosperity and the greater the overcapitalization which
brings on the crisis. Thus the entire periodic cycle is
due to the inability of capitalistic production to satisfy
immediately the social need.[1]

When there is a scarcity of consumption goods, their
price rises; the need for consumption goods excites a
need for capital goods and elevates their price. An excess
or deficiency of consumption goods, though weak, will
give rise to moderate fluctuations in the value of these
goods but to a greater fluctuation in the value of capital

[1] Aftalion, op. cit. pp. 203–207.

goods.[1] The new capital goods must be produced before we can get more consumption goods than existing machinery can manufacture. The manufacturers of consumption goods, attracted by high profits, desire to expand their plants and to multiply their machines. The makers of machines, factories, raw materials, and semi-finished goods buy in turn from other manufacturers. But months and years pass before the new machines and factories are ready to fabricate consumption goods. During this time the need for consumption goods goes unsatisfied. The period of high prices, high profits, and prosperity is prolonged.[2]

Thus it is through the intermediary of *price* and *profits* that the intensity of social wants gives a powerful impulse to production. Prices and profits control production, but as regulating factors they fail to maintain equilibrium because of the long time which in a capitalistic régime separates the beginning of the productive process from the end.[3]

If because of low temperature one wishes to revive the fire, it will take some time before one obtains the desired heat. As the cold persists and as the thermometer con-

[1] Suppose a differential between costs and selling prices of 5 per cent. Then a 5 per cent increase in selling prices will result in a 100 per cent increase in profits, and therefore in a large increase in the value of capital goods.

[2] Aftalion, op. cit. pp. 208, 219. Substantially the same argument was advanced by Professor T. N. Carver six years earlier in his article "A Suggestion for a Theory of Industrial Depressions," *Quarterly Journal of Economics*, May, 1903.

[3] Aftalion, op. cit. p. 209.

tinues to register it, one is likely, if not guided by experience, to put on still more fuel. When at last the fuel begins to burn briskly, the heat will become unbearable. If one is guided by the present sensation of cold and by the indications of the thermometer, one will fatally overheat the room because of the time required before the fuel ignites and the heat circulates through the room. If guided by the thermometer, one will commit a fatal error, but also if one is guided by the present sensation of cold.[1]

It is exactly the same in the economic world. The necessity of consumption goods, the maintenance of high prices and profits, lead the entrepreneur to suppose that the scarcity of capital continues. Thus errors of judgment[2] are caused by the capitalistic, or roundabout, process of production.[3] In the pre-capitalistic civiliza-

[1] Aftalion, op. cit. pp. 209–210.

[2] Pigou lays great stress on errors of judgment, and these he attributes chiefly to the roundabout capitalistic process. He says: "The kernel of the explanation is that optimistic error and pessimistic error, when discovered, give birth to one another in an endless chain, and that the interval between the successive generations is mainly, but not exclusively, determined by the period of gestation of industrial plant and machinery" (*Economics of Welfare* (1st ed.), p. 848). See also Pigou, *Industrial Fluctuations*, pp. 83–84.

[3] See also Taussig, who says that the causes of the larger oscillations are to be found partly in "the time-using or capitalistic method of production." "When there are heavy investments of capital in new enterprises, then the chances of error are greatest, and at the same time a course of error can be persisted in for the longest time without retribution. The railways, so far-reaching in all their industrial effects, have been of the first significance here also. Many of the crises of the nineteenth century were closely associated with excessive or unprofitable

tion price was indeed a good indicator of social wants. In that age the oscillations around the equilibrium proved to be short. Not so in a capitalistic society.

But we must not blame the thermometer — price and profits — too much. Even though these were abolished by a socialistic or communistic order, there would still remain the difficulty of adjusting the capitalistic, or roundabout, process of production to social wants. Profits and prices are not the only deceptive symptoms. It is the *need* itself which misleads and deludes the producers. It is doubtful if leaders in any régime would be able to make a more satisfactory adjustment than entrepreneurs make in the individualistic order.[1]

Now an increase in the demand for consumer's goods gives rise to far greater fluctuations in the demand for fixed capital. Take a purely hypothetical case: an industry requires one hundred thousand looms. The average length of life of these looms is ten years. Then ten thousand looms have to be replaced each year. If, now, the consumers' demand increases 10 per cent, there is an additional need of ten thousand new looms. Thus a 10 per cent increase in consumer demand gives rise to a 100 per cent increase in the demand for fixed capital.[2]

railway building. . . . Not until it [the railway] has been in operation for some years can it be definitely known whether the final increase in enjoyable goods, or human satisfactions, has been such as to justify the large investment " (*Principles of Economics* (1921), Vol. I, pp. 391–392). See also Spiethoff, " Krisen," *Handwörterbuch der Staatswissenschaften* (1925), VI, p. 77.

[1] Aftalion, op. cit. p. 209.

[2] Ibid. p. 220.

The demand for equipment not only fluctuates more violently than the demand for consumption goods but also antedates it, because the demand for the former depends not upon the total volume of the demand for the latter but upon the *rate of growth* of this demand. When the *rate of growth* of demand for consumption goods slackens (even though the demand is still rising, but at a lower rate of increase), the demand for *additional* equipment suffers an absolute decline.[1] If the demand for consumption goods should cease to grow (that is, remain constant) no *additional* equipment will be needed, and the capital producing industries would have nothing to do except to replace and maintain the existing equipment as it wears out.[2] If there should be

[1] Thus the cause *appears* to follow the effect. See C. F. Bickerdike, "A Non-Monetary Cause of Fluctuations in Employment," *Economic Journal*, September, 1914; J. M. Clark, "Business Acceleration and the Law of Demand," *Journal of Political Economy*, 1917; and A. C. Pigou, *Economics of Welfare* (1920).

[2] In all advanced industrial countries there is a tendency for a larger and larger proportion of labor to be absorbed in maintaining and increasing the supply of fixed capital. The relative proportion of labor devoted to maintenance and to new additions to fixed capital is highly significant. Mr. C. F. Bickerdike says that if the time ever came when maintenance alone absorbed all the available energy, the fluctuations would cease. "It is the fact that the stocks are large and yet are being increased that results in violent fluctuations in annual construction" (*Economic Journal*, September, 1914). The business cycle is a function of economic progress. From Bickerdike's point of view it is not so much the capitalistic, or roundabout, process of production, but rather the *elongation* of the process that is responsible for the cycle. Compare also with J. M. Clark's statement that it is largely due to the "fact of large fixed capital that business breeds these calamities for itself out of the laws of its own being" (*The Economics of Overhead Costs*, p. 386).

a slight decline of say 5 per cent in the demand for consumables, it would not even be necessary to replace all the worn-out equipment. If one tenth of the existing equipment wears out each year, then a 5 per cent decline in the demand for consumption goods would reduce the replacement work for the ensuing year to half its former level. On the other hand, an increase in the demand for consumption goods, from the index number of 100 to 110, for example, would result in an increase of 100 per cent in the demand for equipment. Ten thousand *additional* looms would be needed to supply the *new* consumer demand. Since 10,000 looms are needed to replace the worn-out portions of the old equipment, a total of 20,000 looms will be required. If, in the ensuing year, consumer demand rises still further *absolutely*, to the index number 118 (the *rate* of increase having, however, fallen), 8000 more looms will be needed. But only 11,000 looms will be needed to replace the old equipment, and so the total number of looms required will now have fallen to 19,000. Thus, even though consumer demand continues to rise, as soon as the *rate of increase* in consumer demand begins to decline, an absolute decline in the demand for fixed capital ensues.

"Once demand," says Professor J. M. Clark, "starts growing it cannot pause or else the derived demand for means of production will shrink, and when it shrinks, the resulting unemployment will produce a shrinkage in the primary demand. Apparently the interrelations of business are such that a growing demand cannot slacken its growth without bringing on itself an absolute diminution. It must keep on growing in order to stay in the same place!" [1]

The upward movement in the consumption-goods industries causes the upward movement of the capital industries. It is true that the expansion of the capital industries exercises a reflex influence upon consumption. When capital is produced, more workers are employed. The new workers consume a large part of the consumption goods. The rest of the nation have correspondingly less. There follows an insufficiency of wants. Prices rise. During depression the reverse is true: unemployment reduces the purchases of consumption goods, leaving more goods on the market for those who are employed, and so prices fall. Thus the effect reacts upon the cause and reënforces it. But it cannot be doubted, Aftalion thinks, that the first and decisive impulse comes from changes in the demand for consumption goods.[2]

Now what are the forces that produce changes in social wants?[3] First there is the increase in population,

[1] J. M. Clark, *The Economics of Overhead Costs*, p. 390. The University of Chicago Press. See also Cassel, op. cit. pp. 569-570, and W. C. Mitchell, in *The Stabilization of Business* (The Macmillan Company), pp. 24-26.

[2] Aftalion, op. cit. pp. 221-222. This view is precisely the opposite of that expressed by Spiethoff. See *Jahrbuch für Gesetzgebung*, 1903, pp. 692-693; "Krisen," *Handwörterbuch der Staatswissenschaften* (1925), VI, pp. 78-79.

[3] Aftalion's answer, in the main, is that these fluctuations are generated out of prior conditions developed in previous stages in the cycle.

with the attendant increase in social wants and the
desire for more goods. This point is mentioned but not
stressed by Aftalion.[1] The influence of growth of population upon the business cycle is particularly the work
of Pohle.[2] Cassel also gives it considerable weight as
a dynamic factor disturbing the economic equilibrium.
The growth of population creates a demand for fixed
capital. A feeble increase of population and of fixed
capital would, Cassel contends, lessen the business-cycle
movement. A large increase in population and of fixed
capital would give free play to these movements. In this
connection Cassel compares Germany and the United
States with France. The first two exhibit large increases
of population and fixed capital and correspondingly
violent fluctuations of prosperity and depression. On
the other hand, France with her relatively stationary
population has not experienced extreme fluctuations.[3]

[1] Aftalion, op. cit. pp. 215–216.

[2] Cf. Lescure, op. cit. pp. 370–371; Vogel, op. cit. p. 384; Spiethoff,
"Die Krisentheorien von M. v. Tougan-Baranowsky und L. Pohle,"
Jahrbuch für Gesetzgebung, 1903, pp. 704–708. Spiethoff raises the
objection to Pohle's theory that the increase in population is too
steady a factor to cause pronounced upheavals of prosperity and
depression. Moreover, if indeed it could be shown that growth of
population exhibits periodicity, the question would remain whether this
periodicity coincides with the business cycle, and if so, whether it might
not be that the population cycle is result rather than cause. In this
connection see M. B. Hexter, *Social Consequences of Business Cycles*,
pp. 174–175.

[3] Cassel, op. cit. pp. 622–623. Lescure (op. cit. p. 371) argues, on the
other hand, that France has, not less than other countries, been visited
by crises. This is true; but Cassel's point, that the movements have
been less extreme in France, appears to be sound.

The increase in social wants may also proceed from improvements in technique and scientific discoveries. The consequent reduction in cost and therefore of selling prices enlarges consumption and demand.[1]

Moreover, new products are placed on the market; new desires demand satisfaction.[2] The inventive spirit of mankind is directed not solely toward devising new and better technical processes of production but also toward devising new products of an endless variety. These have unusual significance; for while old industries only require an addition to their existing plant when demand increases, new industries require a whole new layout of plant and equipment. Hence new products create an unusual demand for fixed capital. As an example, the automobile industry has given rise to an enormous demand for fixed capital. Once built, it has only to be replaced, in the main, and so when the market is saturated there ensues a great decline in the demand for fixed capital.[3]

Sometimes new products give rise to a shift in demand rather than an increase in demand. Thus it is said that the jewelry industry has suffered a severe decline in demand owing to the rise of the radio industry. Such

[1] Aftalion, op. cit. p. 216.

[2] Ibid. pp. 216–218. It should be noted that Aftalion holds that new wants and technical discoveries are only partial causes, like the disturbances set up by wars and political events.

[3] Similar dislocations are produced by the unequal rate of growth of industries in a progressive society. Cf. E. H. Vogel, *Die Theorie des volkswirtschaftlichen Entwickelungsprozesses und das Krisenproblem*, pp. 343–398.

shifts in demand result in large increases in the demand for fixed capital even though there is no increase in the totality of consumer demand. Assume that the two industries require the same amount of fixed capital. The shift in demand will cut off the replacement demand for fixed capital in the old industry, but it will create a demand for a complete new outlay of fixed capital in the new industry, unless, as is rarely the case, it should be possible to utilize part of the old equipment for the production of the new commodity. It will thus be seen that *shifts* in demand are fully as important as *increases* in demand.

Attention should also be called to the significant influence of wars upon *increases* in demand and *shifts* in demand.[1]

Moreover, tariff *changes* (whether in the direction of higher duties or free trade) are likely to result in transfers of labor and capital from certain industries to other industries. This would call for the building of new outlays of fixed capital. The effect is therefore similar to that caused by shifts in consumer demand.

Allyn Young has emphasized the importance of the changing *distribution* of demand. The explanation of the termination of prosperity he finds "not in a difference between aggregate demand and aggregate supply but in maladjustments of demand and supply. As prices increase the *distribution* as well as the *amount* of money incomes changes, and hence the *incidence* of the demand

[1] Cf. Pigou, *Industrial Fluctuations*, pp. 48–49, 197–198.

for different types of consumption and production goods changes." He shows that in a period of expansion the demand for luxuries increases faster than the demand for necessaries; that prosperous industries attract larger investments, and business surpluses grow faster than the general fund of disposable savings. "The expansion of production does not and cannot shift its direction fast enough to keep pace with the changing distribution of demand. In fact, it advances under its own momentum in such a way as to increase its unfitness to meet the shifting of buyers' demands. In this way strains accumulate in the industrial system which of themselves would bring about its collapse." [1]

Finally, crop fluctuations have an undoubted influence upon consumers' demand. A large harvest decreases the prices of farm products, and so sets free purchasing power for the buyers of these products. This must necessarily result in shifts in demand. Whether large harvests increase or decrease the total purchasing power of farm products depends upon the elasticity of demand for these products as a whole. It is not entirely clear precisely how far crop fluctuations do affect the total purchasing power of farmers, since low prices frequently offset the advantage of large crops.[2] Moreover, the

[1] Allyn A. Young, "The Trend of Prices," *American Economic Review*, Supplement, 1923, p. 11.

[2] Cf. W. M. Persons, *Harvard Review of Economic Statistics*, 1921, pp. 34–36. Among the writers who place more or less emphasis upon harvests as a disturbing factor which upsets economic equilibrium are H. L. Moore, *Economic Cycles* and *Generating Economic Cycles*;

purchasing power of the agricultural population is steadily becoming smaller relative to the total national income.[1] On the other hand, so long as the farms furnish so large a proportion of the raw materials of manufacture, a large harvest and the consequent low *prices* of raw materials can scarcely fail to affect industrial prosperity. Moreover, a large physical volume of crops makes larger demands upon the transportation and storage industries, and this in turn will affect the industries which serve them.

With Aftalion it is not the modern juridical régime (as he puts it) nor the existence of private property that accounts for the recurrence of crises. They spring rather from the whole economic régime, the capitalistic technique, the necessity for preliminary manufacture of capital goods in order to satisfy the demands of consumption, the capitalistic, or roundabout, process of production. These socialism, even, could never pretend to eliminate. It is true that the juridical features influence the cycle. Even Aftalion does not think that the capitalistic technique makes the crisis an inevitable necessity ; rather it makes it quasi-inevitable.[2]

A. C. Pigou, *Economics of Welfare* and *Is Unemployment Inevitable?* (p. 102) ; D. H. Robertson, *A Study of Industrial Fluctuations*, pp. 75–120, 129–155, 165–170, and *Banking Policy and the Price Level*, pp. 14–16; Irving Fisher, "The So-called Business Cycle," *Journal of American Statistical Association*, 1925; G. F. Warren and F. A. Pearson, *The Agricultural Situation*, 1924; L. M. Kovalskaya, *The Problems of Economic Conditions*, Vol. III, Issue I (The Conjuncture Institute, Moscow), p. 166.

[1] Cf. W. C. Mitchell, *Business Annals*, p. 98.

[2] Aftalion, op. cit. p. 257.

CHAPTER V

THE EXCHANGE ECONOMY AS CAUSE OF THE BUSINESS CYCLE

As Jean Lescure has pointed out,[1] the anarchy resulting from the division of the productive process, in an individualistic exchange economy, has been given as a cause of crises by many authors and by different and even opposing schools, such as the classicals and the socialists. Many of the writers whom we have discussed in the preceding chapter have given more or less weight to the complexity of the relationships of an individualistic exchange economy with highly developed specialization and division of labor. In such a society it is difficult to maintain a balanced equilibrium.

Entrepreneurs in a competitive exchange economy cannot possibly have complete knowledge of what the demand will be for their products. Risk and uncertainty are the necessary concomitants of such a régime.[2] Production cannot possibly be adjusted perfectly to the demands of consumers. Division of labor and the exchange economy increases the productivity of labor on the technical side, but it tremendously increases the

---

[1] Lescure, *Des Crises générales et périodiques de surproduction*, p. 358.
[2] Cf. C. O. Hardy, *Risk and Risk-Bearing*; also F. H. Knight, *Risk, Uncertainty and Profit*.

problems of finance and management. Not only must each producer guess as best he can what consumers will want and how much, but he must also adjust his plans to the actions of his competitors. In a primitive economy uncertainty was largely associated with harvests, unusual climatic disturbances, pestilences, wars, etc.; in the modern economy uncertainty is a product of the internal nature of the industrial order.

We have seen that uncertainty springs from the roundabout, capitalistic, time-consuming process of production. But it also arises from the fact that in the modern order products are produced to be exchanged. These two aspects of the modern order are not necessarily coexistent. A thorough-going communistic order would eliminate the exchange economy entirely. An organized order with combinations of the integrated type would eliminate exchange of products in the various stages of production from the raw material to the finished product, but would still retain the exchange of products between industries and between producers and consumers. So also would guild socialism and syndicalism. Collectivism would eliminate all exchange except the sale of products to the final consumer. But all these orders, while modifying or eliminating the competitive exchange economy, would still presumably retain the capitalistic, or roundabout, method of production. The capitalistic process of production is not tied up with a régime of private property and private enterprise, as is, in large part, the individualistic exchange economy.

Among recent writers who have stressed the individualistic exchange economy as a basic factor influencing the business cycle, Lavington [1] is perhaps outstanding. He points out that in the modern economic order there is no central authority to adjust means to ends. Instead, this complex task is left to many thousands of independent entrepreneurs, each one of whom specializes in one small part of the whole vast economic enterprise.[2] The entrepreneur stands at the center of the economic organization. Under his control pass all the productive resources of the community. He estimates future demands and sets resources in motion to meet these demands. If his forecast is optimistic, the producing group which is organized under his command is active, and the market for the products of other groups is improved; if his forecast is pessimistic, the opposite is true. The key to the business situation lies in the mind of the entrepreneur, in the influences which determine his judgments. In such a society errors are bound to arise. And these errors tend to develop cumulatively either in the direction of optimism or of pessimism.[3]

[1] F. Lavington, *The Trade Cycle.* P. S. King & Son, 1922.

[2] Op. cit. pp. 27–28.

[3] See Adolph Löwe, "Wie ist Konjunkturtheorie überhaupt möglich?" (*Weltwirtschaftliches Archiv*, October, 1926), for a brief criticism of the exchange-economy theory. He refers to it as the theory which seeks to "derive the variations of the Konjunktur from the vastness of the modern market as to space, time, and goods, and the misproduction resulting therefrom," and raises the question whether from a presupposed chaos of production a final rhythmical wave movement can arise. For a contrary view see Pigou, *Industrial Fluctuations*, pp. 75–76.

Not only is it difficult for each producer to know what other producers will want, but also each producer is unable to ascertain what all his competitors are doing. This fact is stressed by Beveridge. The demand for a product is met not by one producer but by many, each acting independently of the rest, and each dominated by the desire to do as much business as possible. Since competitors do not know the actions of each other the market is glutted. This is the normal incident of competition.

Every one of ten bootmakers may accurately estimate the total demand for boots, say 10,000 pairs, at the lowest remunerative price. Each of the ten, however, desires to have the supplying of as large a share as possible of this demand — say of a fifth rather than of a tenth. The ten together will therefore set about producing twice as many boots as can be sold at a profit.[1]

Errors of judgment in a society practicing a high degree of division of labor and controlled by separate, specialized entrepreneurs would arise, Pigou tells us, even in a barter economy. A and B each make "at the same time now an exaggerated, now an inadequate estimate of the other's prospective real demand for his stuff. No study of trade cycles can be adequate in which this point is misunderstood."[2]

---

[1] W. H. Beveridge, *Unemployment*, p. 59. Longmans, Green & Co., 1909.

[2] A. C. Pigou, *Is Unemployment Inevitable?* (p. 98). Macmillan & Company, Limited. See also Pigou, *Industrial Fluctuations*, pp. 70–73.

Professor Taussig notes division of labor — the marshaling of different stages in the processes of production — as a factor conditioning the business cycle. Division of labor implies a considerable interval between the first stages of production and the final emergence of the consumable goods. Mistakes are likely to be made, and the errors are not likely to be exposed for a long time.[1]

Two other writers, whose work we shall treat chiefly under the head of the monetary economy theories, have given considerable prominence in their work to the interrelations between the various stages of production. They are Wesley C. Mitchell and Jean Lescure. "The interdependence" of business units is one of the leading threads running through the whole of Mitchell's work. He shows how the diffusion of activity proceeds along the lines of interconnection between enterprises. "One line leads back from the industries first stimulated to the industries which provide raw materials and supplementary supplies. Another line leads forward to the chain of enterprises which handle the increased output of commodities."[2] Lescure advances the view that partial overproduction in certain industries tends to become "generalized" through the interdependence of groups. The crisis in particular industries becomes

[1] F. W. Taussig, *Principles of Economics*, Vol. I, p. 391. The Macmillan Company. See also Alfred Marshall, *Principles of Economics* (Macmillan & Company, Limited, 1916), p. 711.

[2] W. C. Mitchell, *Business Cycles*, p. 453. University of California Press. See also Chapter II of the same book.

generalized through the solidarity of industries. The crisis is born in one particular branch of production and spreads by "repercussion" to all the rest.[1]

The various stages in the productive process (from the raw-material stage up through the various intermediate processes until the goods finally land on the shelves of the retailers) are especially important from the standpoint of the business cycle. The vertical interrelations between producers, in the march from raw materials to the finished product in the hands of the consumer, are of the highest significance.

The product of one stage of the industrial process furnishes the materials for the next stage, and the product of that stage in turn supplies the materials for the next subsequent stage. "Thus the rate of production of one stage cannot long exceed or fall behind that of the stages immediately preceding or following it."[2]

Now in a period of expansion the physical purchases of consumers increase to some extent, but the physical purchases of retailers from wholesalers increase still more, and the physical purchases of wholesalers from manufacturers and of manufacturers from raw-material-producers increase at a still greater rate. The reason is that the dealers and manufacturers all along the line are stocking up with inventories.

[1] Lescure, op. cit. pp. 363–365. See also Veblen, *Theory of Business Enterprise*, pp. 182, 247.

[2] L. K. Frank, "A Theory of Business Cycles," *Quarterly Journal of Economics*, August, 1923, p. 626. See also G. E. Putnam, "Paper Profits and Business Cycles," *Harvard Business Review*, January, 1926.

Obviously this state of affairs cannot go on forever. Eventually the products get dammed up higher and higher, the farther the stage is removed from the consumer. Accordingly purchases are curtailed, and the greater the accumulated stocks, the greater is the curtailment of purchases from the preceding stage. Manufacturers buy less than wholesalers, wholesalers less than retailers, and retailers buy less than consumers. The reason is that each of these groups is supplying the demand from stock. This is the period of depression.[1]

It is now well established that the physical volume of purchases by consumers is surprisingly steady in spite of the fluctuations of the business cycle.[2] Consumers' incomes fluctuate more violently than consumers' purchases. This indicates that wage-earners do not spend as much as they earn during periods of prosperity, and that, on the other hand, they spend more than they earn during periods of depression. This conclusion is in accord with common knowledge and observation. During depression wage-earners live in part from previously accumulated savings and in part they purchase goods from neighborhood stores on credit. During prosperity they pay off their debts and accumulate savings.

[1] Cf. L. K. Frank, op. cit.; also W. I. King, "Business Cycles, their Cause," *American Contractor*, March 3, 1923. See also W. C. Mitchell, *Business Cycles*, pp. 454, 463–464; P. W. Martin, *The Flaw in the Price System* (1926), pp. 98–99.

[2] Cf. W. A. Berridge, *Purchasing Power of the Consumer*, pp. 56–60; L. B. Mann, *Journal of American Statistical Association*, December, 1921; W. C. Mitchell, *Business Cycles*, p. 556; G. Cassel, *A Theory of Social Economy*, pp. 521–526; S. S. Kuznets, *Cyclical Fluctuations*.

Now let us suppose that production could be made to run as even a course as consumption. The fluctuations of business would be greatly reduced. And, indeed, if the fluctuation limits of production were restricted to the rather narrow range of the fluctuations of the retail trade, these latter fluctuations would themselves be reduced thereby, for consumers' incomes would become steadier if production and employment were made steadier, and so consumers' purchases would become more stabilized. Thus, if production fluctuations could be narrowed to the range of the physical purchases of consumers, a force would be set in motion which would *tend* to eliminate the fluctuations entirely. The cyclical movement would tend to run down.

The accumulation of stocks of goods in the several stages of production is responsible for the divergence of physical production from the physical purchases of consumption goods. This accumulation of stocks is due to two factors: first, dealers, wholesalers, and manufacturers place heavier orders for stocks in order to take care of the anticipated increased volume of trade; [1]

[1] Moreover, because of the length of time required to build up a production organization from a condition of low production, retailers find it difficult to get their orders filled; hence they spread out their orders among many firms and deliberately include in their orders a considerable margin over what they expect to get. Manufacturers, in turn, do likewise in ordering raw materials. Finally, as production organizations are brought up to capacity, all buyers are surprised to find orders filled more fully than they had expected. Cf. T. W. Mitchell, "Competitive Illusion as Cause of Business Cycles," *Quarterly Journal of Economics*, August, 1924.

secondly, the increased volume of trade results in higher prices and so leads dealers and manufacturers to make extra heavy purchases of stocks before prices rise still higher.[1] With a slight decline in the physical purchases of consumers the reverse takes place.

After prosperity has been under way for a number of months, a continued increase in the volume of purchases by dealers and manufacturers is checked by limitations of storage space on the one hand and credit to carry the stocks on the other hand. These limitations serve to check the upward movement. These limitations apply particularly to retailers, and so retailers may be said to occupy a strategic position with respect to the interrelations here considered.[2] Hawtrey contends that merchants and dealers are particularly sensitive to credit limitations, a large proportion of their stock being carried by means of credit.

Obviously, production in the preceding stages will tend to be stabilized by a steady, uniform rate of buying on the part of the subsequent stage. If the firms in a certain stage of production face a fairly even demand, steady purchases on their part from the preceding stage will result in a hand-to-mouth policy and small stocks.

[1] Cf. Hudson B. Hastings, *Costs and Profits*, pp. 31–39. Houghton Mifflin Company, 1923.

[2] Cf. Taussig, op. cit. Vol. I, pp. 393–394; W. I. King, op. cit.; L. K. Frank, op. cit.; R. G. Hawtrey, *Good and Bad Trade* (1913), pp. 267–272, and *Monetary Reconstruction* (1923), p. 140; J. M. Clark, *The Economics of Overhead Costs* (1924), pp. 405–406; W. C. Mitchell, *Business Cycles*, p. 454; J. R. Bellerby, *Monetary Stability* (1925), pp. 62–64.

If, on the other hand, the firms in a certain stage face a highly fluctuating demand, steady purchases on their part will necessitate the accumulation of stocks in the dull seasons from which to supply the market in the brisk seasons. The policy of steady uniform purchases may or may not result in the accumulation of stocks, depending upon whether or not the demand in the next succeeding stage is steady or fluctuating. Steady purchases by retailers would result in smaller stocks. On the other hand, steady purchases of raw materials by manufacturers would result in large accumulation of stocks if the purchases of wholesalers continued to fluctuate.

Retailers, wholesalers, and manufacturers are more likely to pursue a hand-to-mouth policy if the price level is stabilized or slowly falling. In recent years the accumulated stocks in American industries have been running along on a relatively low level. Probably also the memory of the large stocks held in 1920–1921 and of the disastrous consequences is a potent factor in the situation. With the speculative accumulation of stocks largely eliminated, production is on the whole steadier than it would otherwise be. Certain industries, however, like railroads, with a fluctuating demand, could help to stabilize production still more if they would budget their requirements for a year or so in advance and so stabilize their orders.[1]

---

[1] Cf. editorial on "Hand to Mouth Buying," in *New Republic*, September 29, 1926; see also *Business Bulletin*, The Cleveland Trust Company, November 15, 1926.

It is probably with respect to this matter of a steady volume of purchases that installment buying has its chief social significance. If installment buying has the effect of inducing consumers "to pledge so large a portion of their future incomes that they must subsequently restrict their purchases the very basis of steady output is broken." [1]

It is evident that the interrelations between the various stages in the productive process are of great significance from the standpoint of cyclical fluctuations. It is therefore not to be wondered at that many writers have looked to the combination movement as a stabilizing factor.[2] Integration of industries is clearly of special importance. But horizontal combinations may have the effect of encouraging speculative purchases and thus intensifying business fluctuations. If such combinations stabilize the prices of basic materials while selling prices generally are rising, the speculative tendency will be encouraged.[3]

[1] *New Republic*, as above.

[2] Cf. Abraham Berglund, *Quarterly Journal of Economics*, November, 1923, and August, 1924; E. H. Vogel, *Die Theorie des volkswirtschaftlichen Entwickelungsprozesses und das Krisenproblem*, pp. 388–394; T. B. Veblen, *The Theory of Business Enterprise*, pp. 258–266; E. M. H. Lloyd, *Stabilization*, pp. 87–113; Robert Liefmann, *Allgemeine Volkswirtschaftslehren* (1924), p. 69; Emil Lederer, "Konjunktur und Krisen," *Grundriss der Sozialökonomik*, IV, i (1925), pp. 409–411.

[3] D. H. Robertson, *Banking Policy and the Price Level*, pp. 99–103; D. H. MacGregor, *Economic Journal*, December, 1924, pp. 639–640.

CHAPTER VI

THE MONEY ECONOMY AS CAUSE OF THE BUSINESS CYCLE

We have noted three outstanding characteristics of the modern economic order: (1) the unequal distribution of wealth, (2) the capitalistic, or roundabout, process of production, (3) the interdependence of enterprises in an exchange economy based on division of labor. The modern industrial system is also characterized by the fact that it is a money economy. "Economic activity takes the form of making and spending money incomes." [1] This characteristic of the modern order has received much emphasis in the literature of the business cycle, and to these writers we now turn our attention.

It should be noted that a money economy presupposes necessarily an exchange economy, while on the other hand it is possible to have an exchange economy without a money economy. The money-economy theory necessarily deals with an exchange relationship, but the exchange emphasized is not that of goods against goods, but of money against goods. It is this that distinguishes the money economy from the exchange economy. The writers who emphasize the money economy do not

[1] W. C. Mitchell, *Business Cycles*, p. 21. University of California Press.

131

overlook the fact that the producers of a community provide for each other's wants through an elaborate coöperative process, but they hold that the productive process is "brought into dependence upon factors which have but a remote connection with the national conditions of well-being — factors which determine the prospects of making money." [1]

There are two lines of thought which approach the problem of the business cycle from the standpoint of the money economy. One — starting with H. Thornton in his *Enquiry into the Nature and Effects of the Paper Credit of Great Britain*, published in 1802, and continuing through the writings, among others, of Ricardo, Juglar, Sidgwick, Giffen, Marshall, Wicksell, Fisher, and finally culminating in Hawtrey — runs in terms of the cyclical short-run fluctuations of prices and the interrelations of the discount rate, the real rate of interest (or the rate of profit), and the general level of prices. The other — starting, as far as the present writer can discover, with Veblen in his *Theory of Business Enterprise*, published in 1904, and developed more fully by Lescure and especially by Wesley C. Mitchell — runs in terms of the interrelations of costs and selling prices, profit margins and capitalization. The first views the business cycle in terms of rising and falling prices and raises the question What are the causes that account for these price cycles of which the business cycle essentially consists? The second views the business cycle in

[1] Cf. Mitchell, op. cit. p. 22.

terms of profit margins and raises the question What are the causes of these fluctuating profit margins, the lags of costs behind selling prices, the maladjustments of net income and capitalization, which constitute essentially the cycle? In a sense the former seeks to explain why price cycles occur; the latter seeks to explain why these price cycles make business alternately prosperous and depressed.

Thornton pointed out that the demand for bank loans will depend upon two circumstances: (1) the amount of interest to be paid on the sum borrowed and (2) the mercantile or other gain to be obtained by the employment of borrowed capital. "We may, therefore, consider this question as turning principally on a comparison of the rate of interest taken at the bank with the current rate of mercantile profit."[1]

The borrowers, in consequence of that artificial state of things which is produced by the law against usury, obtain their loans too cheap. . . . The temptation to borrow, in time of war, too largely at the bank, arises, as has been observed, from the high rate of mercantile profit. Capital is then scarce, and the gain accruing from the employment of it is proportionally considerable.[2]

From Ricardo we have the following:

The applications to the bank for money then depend on the comparison between the rate of profits that may be

[1] H. Thornton, *An Enquiry into the Nature and Effects of the Paper Credit of Great Britain* (1802), p. 287.

[2] Ibid. pp. 288–289.

made by the employment of it and the rate at which they are willing to lend it. If they charge less than the market rate of interest there is no amount of money which they might not lend. If they charge more than that rate none but spendthrifts and prodigals will be found to borrow of them.[1]

Clement Juglar [2] related gold flows with cyclical price fluctuations. Changes in the quantity of money affect prices only because they affect interest rates, and these in turn affect the volume of credit and so prices.[3] The discount rate and the prospective rate of industrial profit conditions the volume of credit and hence the price level. The discount rate and the prospective rate of profit determine the volume of commercial transactions, and these create the basic commercial paper upon which the credit of banks is issued. Bank credit results from business transactions rather than gives birth to them.[4]

Along similar lines Sidgwick tells us that banks can undoubtedly *enable merchants to act* on mistaken *beliefs* that goods are, or are about to be, worth more in gold

[1] David Ricardo, *Principles of Political Economy* (1817), Gonner's edition, pp. 351–352. J. Bell & Sons, 1903.

[2] According to Schumpeter, Juglar was the first to see clearly that the crises is merely a phase of a process. He saw that the expansion was the cause of the depression. Cf. Schumpeter, "Die Wellenbewegung des Wirtschaftslebens," *Archiv für Sozialwissenschaft*, 1914, pp. 2–3, 6–7. Juglar's *Des Crises commerciales* was first published in 1860.

[3] Cf. J. W. Angell, *The Theory of International Prices*, pp. 237, 277. Harvard University Press.

[4] Cf. J. R. Commons, H. L. McCracken, and W. E. Zeuch, *Review of Economic Statistics* (1922), p. 261.

than will prove to be the case. In consequence merchants make extended purchases and raise prices. In this way banks render possible alternations of inflated and depressed prices, which would not occur if everything were paid for in hard coin and no credit were given. And even if merchants gave credit, as at present, these fluctuations would not be so marked were it not for the possibility that the banking system affords of increasing the generally accepted medium of exchange.[1]

An increased supply of gold must pass through the banks and so increase their lending power. Hence the rate of discount will tend to fall, and this fall will tend to cause increased borrowing, an extended use of the medium of exchange, and so a rise in prices. "Thus the fall in the purchasing power of money, consequent on an influx of gold, will normally establish itself through an antecedent and connected fall in the value of the use of money."[2]

Robert Giffen proposed to set out the reasons for the special importance of the supply of gold from the mines, in connection with two questions; namely, the rate of discount and the level of general prices. First it should be noted that the rate of discount and the level of prices are interdependent. A rise in prices tends to make "money" in demand and thus raise discount rates; a fall makes "money" abundant and lowers rates. Simi-

[1] Henry Sidgwick, *The Principles of Political Economy*. Macmillan & Company, Limited, 1883. Cf. 3d. ed., pp. 249–250.
[2] Ibid. pp. 254–255.

larly, a change in the discount rate affects prices. A
rise tends to lower prices; a fall tends to raise them.
"There is incessant action and reaction." [1]

An excess of lending tends to raise prices. Borrowers
borrow in order to purchase or avoid selling. Hence
prices rise. Wages in turn rise, and with their rise the
requirements for small change are increased and the
banking reserve trenched upon. Thus, when there is
borrowing, a bank's liabilities are increased at the very
time that a cause is in operation tending to diminish
the reserve. On the other hand, when borrowing
diminishes, banking liabilities also diminish and the
reserve tends to increase. The one instrument that a
banker possesses to check borrowing when his liabilities
increase and his reserve diminishes is to raise the rate of
discount. The higher rates of discount check, in turn, the
rise in prices which the borrowing has produced. The
banker's loans are now paid off, his liabilities diminish,
and so prices and wages fall. Reserves now accumulate
in the banks, and this compels a lowering of rates until
borrowing begins again and prices and wages rise. [2]

What appears to happen is that when cash is added to
the banking reserve it acts at first on the rate of discount,
and tends to produce the addition required to the circulating capital of the country; but the supply of cash for
small change being only obtainable from the banking re-

[1] Robert Giffen, *Essays in Finance*, pp. 38–39. G. P. Putnam's Sons,
1886.
[2] Ibid. pp. 49–50.

serve, the reserve in turn is trenched upon and the addition to the bank's liabilities is checked.[1]

With increasing population and production the aggregate deposits and liabilities of banks must increase and consequently a larger and larger reserve will be required. "If no such reserve is forthcoming, then equilibrium can only be restored by a decline in nominal values, which must be brought about, if necessary, by a raising of the rates of discount."[2] Moreover, the increase in numbers and wealth implies a larger requirement for cash as small change, and this trenches further upon bank reserves and so contributes to the increase in discount rates and the fall in prices. "To maintain equilibrium in the complex system, therefore, a steady addition to the stock of cash is required."[3]

Marshall[4] and Wicksell[5] made similar analyses. Wicksell's views on this subject we have already summarized in Chapter IV. If the bank discount rate is below the real rate of interest, borrowing is stimulated and

[1] Ibid. p. 51. This statement is of the highest significance for Hawtrey's theory, which we discuss later.

[2] Ibid. p. 53.

[3] Ibid. p. 53.

[4] In his testimony before the Gold and Silver Commission of 1887–1888. Cf. Alfred Marshall, *Official Papers*, pp. 49–52, *Money, Credit and Commerce*, p. 45, and *Principles of Economics* (7th ed.), pp. 593–595; Bertil Ohlin, *Economic Journal*, September, 1926, p. 506; J. W. Angell, *The Theory of International Prices*, p. 133.

[5] The only English statement by Wicksell is his article on "The Influence of the Rate of Interest on Prices," *Economic Journal*, 1907, but he had published a similar analysis in German as early as 1897. Cf. Ohlin, *Economic Journal*, 1926, p. 505.

prices rise. If the bank discount rate is above the real interest rate, borrowing is curtailed and prices fall.

In his *Purchasing Power of Money* Fisher [1] puts forward the interest rate as the regulator of expansion and contraction. It is the tardiness of the rise in the interest rate (that is, the rate on loans) that is responsible for the expansion. But the rise in interest though belated is progressive, and as soon as it overtakes the rate of rise in prices [2] the whole situation is changed. The banks are forced in self-defense to raise the rate in order to protect their reserves. As soon as the rate becomes adjusted, borrowers can no longer hope to make great profits, and so the demand for loans ceases to expand. Prices stop rising; but the rate of interest continues to rise still further for a time, because the mistake of over-borrowing compels the victims to borrow still further to protect their solvency. But the banks now hesitate to lend except on the best security. Loans are contracted, and prices fall. [3]

These oscillations have their origin in some initial disturbance which upsets the equilibrium. [4] The extra-

[1] Irving Fisher, *The Purchasing Power of Money*. The Macmillan Company, 1911.

[2] Hawtrey contends that it is not necessary that the rate of discount should overtake the rate of rise in prices in order to check inflation. See discussion of Hawtrey's position below.

[3] Fisher, op. cit. pp. 64, 70.

[4] Compare Wicksell's statement with Fisher's. Fisher thinks of the profit rate as a resultant of the movement of the price level (op. cit. p. 73), whereas Wicksell thinks of the price level as the resultant of any divergence that may arise between the discount rate and the profit rate.

neous force in question may be an increase in the quantity of money, large crops, or inventions.[1]

This brings us to Hawtrey,[2] whose theory of the business cycle may be said to be the culmination of the line of analysis which we have been tracing. Earlier writers (with the exception of Fisher) gave only incidental notice to the problem of the business cycle. Hawtrey applied the analysis of his predecessors directly to the trade cycle, and found in this analysis of the interrelations and interactions of reserves, discount rates, bank credit, prices, and money drawn into hand-to-hand circulation the complete explanation of the periodic fluctuations in modern industry and trade.

Hawtrey takes the position that there is an inherent tendency toward fluctuations in the money economy, with its existing banking institutions and practices.[3] So long as credit is regulated with reference to reserve proportions the trade cycle is bound to recur. The flow of legal-tender money into circulation and back is one of the very tardiest consequences of a credit expansion or contraction. If the central bank waits for this flow to affect its reserves, and sits passively looking on at an expansion or contraction gathering impetus before it takes any decisive action, we cannot escape from

[1] Fisher, op. cit. p. 70; see also Pigou, *Industrial Fluctuations*, pp. 91–99.

[2] *Good and Bad Trade* (1913), *Currency and Credit* (1919), *Monetary Reconstruction* (1923), and *The Economic Problem* (1925).

[3] R. G. Hawtrey, *Good and Bad Trade*, p. 199. Constable Company, Limited.

the alternations of feverish activity with depression and unemployment.[1]

The periodicity of expansions and contractions of credit which has long attracted the attention of economists is, Hawtrey tells us, the natural result of the slow response of peoples' cash balances to credit movements. Credit expansion is not immediately accompanied by a proportionate increase in the earnings of the working classes or in their power to absorb cash. When earnings do increase, they go to a great extent not into increased balances, but into increased expenditure. In so far as the money paid out on one pay day comes back through the shops to the banks by the next, no additional strain is put upon bank reserve. But as earnings rise, there begins a gradual accretion of people's cash balances, which will continue until these balances are in due proportion to the increased earnings. But this process takes a considerable time. The increase in balances lags behind the increase in earnings. Credit increases, then earnings, and finally the cash balances of people. When earnings reach the maximum, the cash portion of the "unspent margin" is still short of the level corresponding to this maximum. "The wage-earners are still absorbing more money than they spend." This creates a drain on the bank reserves. Finally the current is reversed, and money returns to the banks. But the depletion of people's cash reserves is gradual and con-

[1] R. G. Hawtrey, *Monetary Reconstruction*, p. 145. Longmans, Green & Co.

tinues long after the banks have ceased to contract credit. Thus there accumulates an excess of cash in the banks, which provides opportunity for a renewed credit expansion.[1]

It is this lag of cash balances in the hands of the people which automatically swings the pendulum and keeps the industrial mechanism constantly oscillating up and down.[2] An overaccumulation of bank reserves induces bankers to lower the rate of discount below the profit rate, and so borrowing is encouraged. Prices rise, then wages, but a period of time elapses before an appropriate amount of cash is drawn out into hand-to-hand circulation. Bankers do not realize that they have overexpanded until this drain of cash from the banks severely

[1] R. G. Hawtrey, *Currency and Credit*, pp. 125–126. Longmans, Green & Co.

[2] If an "increase or decrease of credit money promptly brought with it a proportionate increase or decrease in the demand for cash, the banks would no longer either drift into a state of inflation or be led to carry the corresponding process of contraction unnecessarily far" (*Good and Bad Trade*, p. 266). Compare with the analysis of the money mechanism under the national banking system by Allyn A. Young in *Review of Economic Statistics* (1925). This study brings out the interrelations of the New York money market and the interior. "Loans and deposits expand in New York because money has flowed there." "But a considerable part of the funds thus secured in New York could not be held there long. Payments had to be made to the *ultimate* borrowers in other parts of the country. Deposits were transferred to outside banks. The revival of industrial activity with which these outside payments probably had something to do, led to increased lending by outside banks. An increase of prices and of the volume of trade draws money from New York, through the banks, into circulation. Just how far these movements would go without reversing themselves appears to have depended upon a general conjuncture of circumstances. I see no basis for the belief that these

reduces bank reserves. At this point bankers conclude
that the amount of credit money in existence is more
than they think prudent, having regard to their holdings
of cash, and so they raise the rate of discount above the
profit rate. Dealers accordingly reduce their stocks by
giving fewer orders to producers. Prices fall, but wages
lag behind, and people's cash balances lag still more.
When cash finally does begin to flow back to the banks
in large volume, it is found (too late) that the credit
contraction has been excessive, since there now develops
an overaccumulation of cash reserves. The banks must
get rid of this excess. They lower the discount rate below the prospective profit rate, and so another period of
inflation ensues. Were it not for the *lag of cash balances*
and the consequent alternating excess and deficiency of
bank reserves, a stable equilibrium might be reached.[1]
"The too ready acceptance of reserve proportions as the
guide to credit policy was the real cause of the trade
cycle before the war." [2] In the interrelations of reserves,
cash balances, discount rates, and the profit rate [3] is to

cyclical swings, once under way, were never halted until the resources of
the banks had been exhausted. Monetary factors undoubtedly have
much to do with the cyclical fluctuations of business activities. Moreover, they set limits beyond which such fluctuations cannot go. But
only in cycles of exceptional magnitude do such limits become effective."
See also Albert Hahn, "Zur Frage des volkswirtschaftlichen Erkenntnisinhalts der Bankbilanzziffern," *Vierteljahrsheften zur Konjunkturforschung*," 1. Jahrgang, 1926, Ergänzungsheft 4.

[1] Hawtrey, *Good and Bad Trade*, pp. 267–272.

[2] Cf. *Economic Journal*, June, 1926, p. 330.

[3] Cf. Alvin H. Hansen, *Cycles of Prosperity and Depression* (1921),
pp. 104–110.

be found, then, the mechanism which produces the oscillations of expansion and contraction.[1]

If, on the other hand, the central banks would watch, not the reserve proportions but the flow of purchasing power, early action could then be taken.

It is the *flow* of purchasing power that is important, not the outstanding aggregate of money units.[2] The "unspent margin," in terms of money units, is made up of the money in circulation and the bank credits outstanding.[3] The unspent margin of real purchasing

[1] In this connection it should also be noted that even though trade were temporarily stable and the discount rate were equal to the profit rate, if for any reason the profit rate deviates from the rate of interest charged on loans, the discrepancy between them tends to be enlarged. If the profit rate happens to be slightly higher, there will be an increased demand for loans, a consequent increase in purchasing power, and so prices rise, which would still further increase the profit rate. Thus equilibrium is essentially unstable in the sense that any slight deviation of the two rates will tend to grow greater and greater until steps are taken to correct it. "This of itself shows that the money market must be subject to fluctuations" (*Good and Bad Trade*, p. 76). Credit is "by nature unruly. It is always straining at its tether, or rather, it is perpetually starting to run away, and then is being pulled up with a jerk when the limit of inflation consistent with the maintenance of the metallic standard is reached" (*Currency and Credit*, p. 127).

[2] Hawtrey, *Monetary Reconstruction*, pp. 145, 120. "Stagnant cash balances are a characteristic of periods of trade depression. When trade is profitable dealers cannot afford to let money lie idle, but when every transaction threatens, under the stress of falling markets, to end in a loss, idle balances are allowed to mount up" (p. 119).

[3] Hawtrey, *Currency and Credit*, p. 35. Note the following from Allyn A. Young: "The more rapidly the unspent margin increases, the *slower* will be the advance of prices. A rise of prices results from the use of purchasing power, not from its accumulation" (*Quarterly Journal of Economics*, 1920, p. 525).

power equates to the command over wealth which the
people hold in reserve.[1] Hawtrey's "command over
wealth which the people hold in reserve" appears to
be similar to J. M. Keynes's "volume of real balances,"
the K and K' in his equation $n = p(K + rK')$.[2] The
volume of real balances may fluctuate violently even
though there is little change in the volume of cash or
in the reserve policy of the banks.

The characteristic of the credit cycle (as the alternation
of boom and depression is now described) consists in a
tendency of K and K' to diminish during the boom and
increase during the depression irrespective of changes in
n and r, these movements representing respectively a
diminution and an increase of "real" balances (that is,
balances, in hand or at the bank, measured in terms of
purchasing power) ; so that we might call this phenomenon
deflations and inflations of real balances.[3]   "Cyclical

[1] Hawtrey, *Currency and Credit*, p. 39.

[2] $K =$ the number of consumption units, the monetary equivalent of
which the public find it convenient to keep in "cash"; $K' =$ the number
of consumption units, the monetary equivalent of which the public find
it convenient to keep in bank balances; $p =$ the price of each consumption unit, or the index number of prices; $n =$ the number of units of
"cash" in circulation; $r =$ the proportion of their potential liabilities to
the public which the banks keep in "cash." Cf. *Economic Journal*,
March, 1924, p. 65.

[3] J. M. Keynes, *Monetary Reform*, p. 91. Harcourt, Brace and Company. See also Marshall, *Money, Credit, and Commerce*, pp. 43–48. See
also Hawtrey, *Monetary Reconstruction*, p. 120. Hawtrey notes that in
England prices were deflated 50 per cent without any visible fall in
bank deposits. Röpke remarks that the delay in the use of money
balances "comes to the aid of other money owners who make use of the
unspent margin" ("Kredit and Konjunktur," *Jahrbücher für Nationalökonomie und Statistik*, 1926, p. 249).

fluctuations are characterized, not primarily by changes in n or r, but by changes in K and K'." [1]

Under the conditions of uncontrolled banking institutions the discount rate is regulated by the cash reserves of the banks, and so it acts too tardily to check the inflation and deflation. Hawtrey would raise and lower the discount rate earlier and so stabilize the flow of purchasing power and the price level. Pigou has pointed out that such a discount policy would differ from the present practice "not in the fact that the discount rate would be moved up in booms (and correspondingly down in depressions), but only in respect of the *time*

[1] Keynes, op. cit. p. 95. In this connection it is of interest to note the "income theory" of money and prices suggested by Wieser in a communication to the Verein für Socialpolitik in 1909 and developed by Aftalion in his article "Les Expériences monétaires récentes et la théorie du revenu," *Revue d'économie politique*, May–June, 1925. See also his "Théorie psychologique de la monnaie," *Revue d'économie politique*, July–August, 1925. Aftalion remarks that price fluctuations depend upon the respective movements of the *money* income and of the *real* income. If the first increases while the second is stationary, the price rises. This is what happens in a period of inflation (May–June issue of *Revue*, pp. 839–840). $R = PQ$ (R being the money income, P the price level, and Q the total production). This theory has the advantage that it squares with the modern theory of value with its supply-and-demand schedules. Instead of "supply of money" being given in terms of the existing quantity of money, as the quantity theory has it, the income theory offers money-supply schedules, which, in fact, are only the demand schedules for goods. As the money income increases, the money-supply schedules fall, which means that the demand schedules for goods rise. One is disposed to pay more for goods if he feels himself richer; if, in fact, his money income is increased. Instead of viewing the problem mechanistically, as the quantity theory does, the income theory is able to say why buyers and sellers act as they do. The income theory substitutes the explanation of *men* for the explanation of *things*. It

at which, and the *extent to* which, the rate of discount would be changed." [1]

But, it may be asked, is the discount rate really a sufficiently powerful regulator of the price cycle? Hawtrey contends that it is. How can a slight change of 1 or 2 per cent in the rate of interest on temporary loans have such far-reaching results? The explanation is in part to be found in the immediate reaction on merchants, and these, in Hawtrey's view, occupy a strategic place in the business mechanism. It is perfectly true, says Hawtrey, that the producer is not much troubled by the rate of interest he has to pay his banker. [2] But that is not so in the case of the merchant or dealer, who is constantly carrying stocks of goods large in proportion to his own capital, and who makes very nice calculations as to his margin of profit and the cost of borrowing. A moderate rise in the cost of borrowing will make the

attaches itself to the incomes of individuals and the psychological effect of these variations on price. It does not forget that economic movements are imputable to our desires, our aspirations, our wants; that economic laws ought to be explained through the behavior of human beings. It substitutes psychological motives for mechanical and external necessities (May–June issue of *Revue*, pp. 820–823).

The effect of an increase of incomes upon price will be different, depending on who the individuals are who are benefited. What kind of people have had their incomes raised? rich or poor? savers or spenders? demanders of luxuries or demanders of necessities? The increase of income does not affect the price mechanically or automatically, but through the desires of those whose incomes are raised (May–June issue of *Revue*, pp. 824–825).

[1] Pigou, in *Is Unemployment Inevitable?* (p. 115).

[2] Compare with Snyder, *American Economic Review*, December, 1925, and W. F. Mitchell, *American Economic Review*, June, 1926.

carrying of stocks appreciably less attractive to him. He will buy less and sell more, and so a fall in prices is started.[1] The problem of regulating prices is reduced to the problem of regulating trade borrowing, and the volume of trade borrowing can be controlled by the discount rate.[2]

But suppose prices are rising rapidly. How can a relatively slight rise in the discount rate check the tendency to buy with a view to the advance in prices? Hawtrey's answer is that it is not the *past* rise in prices, but the *future* rise that has to be counteracted. It is a pyschological problem. "To the trader the high rate of interest presents itself in the first instance as an expense to be subtracted from his profits, but behind this initial loss looms the far more serious menace of a difficulty in borrowing, which will affect not merely himself but those to whom he hopes to sell."[3] As soon as the rate is high enough to offset the trader's prospects of *future* profits, it becomes deterrent. The rise in the discount rate discourages buying and encourages selling. Once deflation is started, the holding of commodities in stock means an actual loss. The fall of prices reënforces the original process. Once the high discount rate has become deterrent at all, it tends to grow more and more deterrent. Thus mighty changes can be wrought by relatively slight changes in the discount rate.[4]

[1] *Monetary Reconstruction*, p. 140; *Currency and Credit*, p. 124.
[2] *Monetary Reconstruction*, pp. 139, 143.
[3] *Currency and Credit*, p. 128.
[4] *Monetary Reconstruction*, pp. 108, 111.

The discount rate, then, influences particularly the actions of dealers, and fluctuations in dealers' purchases are at the center of business fluctuations. When dealers proceed to reduce their stocks and give fewer orders to producers, production is curtailed, unemployment ensues, earnings decline, and purchases are reduced. The movement thus spreads from the dealers to the rest of the community and back again, and so reënforces itself.[1]

Thus, in Hawtrey's view the unregulated money and banking mechanism produce in an unceasing round the alternating rise and decline in prices and consequently prosperity and depression.[2] A fall in prices forces the producer either to reduce output or to reduce the cost of production. If he chooses the first horn of the dilemma, unemployment ensues, and so business depression; if he chooses the second, wages, salaries, interest, rents, or profits must be lowered. Interest on borrowed funds is a fixed charge, and it cannot be reduced unless the business actually becomes insolvent. Profits will likely first be encroached upon. But if the margin of profit is narrow, there is no recourse except to lower wages or dismiss some of the employees. If wages are lowered sufficiently, production might be maintained, but the consequent redistribution of the national income would

---

[1] Hawtrey, *Good and Bad Trade*, pp. 267–268.
[2] Cf. Irving Fisher, "Our Unstable Dollar and the So-called Business Cycle," *Journal of the American Statistical Association*, June, 1925.

at least entail a necessary shift in production.[1] However, wages cannot in point of fact be lowered except by the pressure of distress. Thus, unemployment being the inevitable whip by which labor is forced to accept lower wages, the readjustment to a lower price level cannot be accomplished except by passing through a period of depression. Nor can the fixed charges be reduced except by the pressure of insolvency. If the habits of the people could be adapted without delay to the change, the production of wealth might continue unabated in spite of a fall in prices. But customary wages, rents, interest, and profits exert such a profound influence upon men's minds that the readjustment can in point of fact not be made except under the pressure of such distress as is experienced in periods of depression.[2]

[1] Hawtrey, op. cit. pp. 40-41. It should be noted that no account is taken in this analysis of the fact that reduction of cost of production might be accomplished by increasing the efficiency of the productive factors without decreasing the money incomes at all. But such changes are of a long-run sort and cannot be applied rapidly enough to meet the shifts in money-purchasing power, which cause, as Hawtrey sees it, the fluctuations in prices. The only adjustment that can be made to declines of prices, then, is one that runs in terms of reduced money costs.

[2] This argument reminds one of Veblen's statement that depression is a "malady of the affections." "The discrepancy which discourages business men is a discrepancy between that nominal capitalization which they have set their hearts upon through habituation in the immediate past and that actual capitalizable value of their property which its current earning capacity will warrant. But where the preconceptions of the business men engaged have, as commonly happens, in great part, been fixed and legalized in the form of interest-bearing securities, this malady of the affections becomes extremely difficult to remedy" (*The Theory of Business Enterprise*, pp. 237-238). Mill

We turn now to the second group of money-economy theories. The emphasis here is upon costs and selling prices, profit margins, and capitalization.

Veblen [1] finds that depression and prosperity are phenomena of price disturbance, either of decline or advance. They affect industry because industry is managed on a business footing, in terms of price and for the sake of profits.[2] Instead of approaching the problem from the side of the industrial phenomena, the mechanical facts of production and consumption, Veblen approaches it from the side of business enterprise — the phenomena of price, earnings, and capitalization.[3]

expresses a somewhat similar view as follows: " ... there is hardly any amount of business which may not be done, if people will be content to do it on small profits" (*Principles of Political Economy*, pp. 561–562).

[1] Thorstein B. Veblen, *The Theory of Business Enterprise*. Charles Scribner's Sons, 1904.

[2] Veblen, like Tougan-Baranowsky, appears to have got his inspiration in part from Karl Marx. In Volume III, chap. xv, of *Capital*, Marx says: "It must never be forgotten that the production of this surplus-value ... is the immediate purpose and the compelling motive of capitalist production. It will not do to represent capitalist production as something which it is not, that is to say, as a production having for its immediate purpose the consumption of goods, or the production of means of enjoyment for capitalists." The capitalist mode of production "comes to a standstill at a point determined by the production and realization of profit, not by the satisfaction of social needs." "The rate of profit is the compelling power of capitalist production, and only such things are produced as yield a profit." "What worries Ricardo is the fact that the rate of profit, the stimulating principle of capitalist production, the fundamental pressure and driving force of accumulation, should be endangered by the development of production itself."

[3] Veblen, op. cit. pp. 180, 185. "It [the interrelation of industries] is a pecuniary relation, in the last resort a price relation, and the balance of this system of interstitial relations is a price balance" (p. 188).

An era of prosperity is an era of rising prices, and when prices cease to rise, prosperity is on the wane. An advance in prices may be born of a speculative movement due to circumstances extraneous to the industrial process, such as a war, an unusual crop, or a new tariff law; or it may spring from an increased supply of precious metals, an inflation of the currency, or a more efficient use of credit instruments.[1]

Rising prices bring larger earnings due to the differential gain in increased selling price of the output over the expenses of production. As soon as this differential advantage ceases, the era of prosperity enters on its closing phase. Such differential advantage arises mainly from two causes : First, the lines of industry which are remote, industrially speaking, from the point of initial disturbances, are less promptly and acutely affected by the price rise. This retardation means that the industries near the seat of disturbance can, for a time, draw cheap supplies from the remote industries. Secondly, the chief and most secure differential advantage is that due to the relatively slow advance in wages.[2]

Presently the expenses of production overtake or nearly overtake the prospective selling price.[3] The

[1] Ibid. pp. 235, 251, 194. The "potent fact which serves as an incentive to the acceleration of business is a rise of prices. This rise of prices ... takes its start from some specific initial disturbance of prices. That is to say, prices rise first in some one industry or line of industries" (p. 194).

[2] Ibid. pp. 199–120.

[3] "Increasing wages cut away the surest ground of that differential price advantage on which an era of prosperity runs" (ibid. p. 212).

differential advantage fails, and the rate of earnings falls off. It is then discovered that the capitalization (which was conservative while the earning capacity rested on a large differential advantage) now proves excessive after the earning capacity has declined. There follows a shrinkage of values to a point where the collateral will not support the credit extension of contracts and loans built upon the basis of the former high earnings. If the claims are pressed, there is no recourse except through forced sales or bankruptcy. The forced sale of products drives prices down, lessens the profits of competitors, and, in turn, throws them into the class of insolvents. Thus the movement spreads from firm to firm. The industrial crisis is a period of shrinkage of values and of capitalization.[1]

It is this aspect of Veblen's theory — the interrelations of costs and selling prices and the consequent necessary readjustment of capitalization to the altered net earnings — that has permanent value.[2] And it is this that is carried forward and developed by Lescure and Mitchell.

[1] Ibid. pp. 191–192, 201–205. See Marx, *Capital*, Vol. III, chap. xv.

[2] Veblen's generalization, that the improvements of the modern machine industry are constantly affecting the cost of goods more than they affect the value of money metals, and so prices tend to fall, has certainly been proved erroneous by the logic of events. It was this generalization which led him to the conclusion that under the modern machine industry the cost of production was constantly being lowered too rapidly to permit a reduction of capitalization sufficient to allow a "reasonable" rate of profit, and that therefore depression was normal to the modern industrial situation. See also Robert Liefmann (*Allgemeine Volkswirtschaftslehre*, p. 70), who contends that inventions, by rendering machinery obsolete before it is amortized, produces depression.

In our modern society, says Lescure, profit plays the rôle of motivating the entrepreneur. The entrepreneur ceases to produce when the margin between cost and selling price becomes too narrow. At the end of a period of prosperity the cost rises in certain essential industries more rapidly than price. Industries are obliged to pay a high price for equipment and construction and a high rate of interest on borrowed capital. Wages rise, and the work is of a poorer quality.[1]

Toward the end of a period of inflation the rise of costs ceases to be compensated by a rise of the selling price in most industries. In modern societies the industries which absorb the most capital sell their products at a price more or less fixed. Railroads, tramways, electricity, are examples.[2] In shipping, freight rates are established frequently by a pooling agreement; shipping rates fluctuate less than the general price level. Building rates change very slowly. Finally, with respect to manufacturing generally, in so far as new factories and equipment enter the market, the output of goods is increased, and this tends to check the rise in prices.[3] But this augmentation of production is not the essential phenomenon. The important factor is the contraction of demand, and the high cost is here the

[1] Lescure, *Des Crises générales et périodiques de surproduction* (1923 ed.), p. 386. The first edition was published in 1907 by the Librairie de la société du Recueil Sirey.

[2] Ibid. p. 393. Mitchell is cited on this point in the 1923 edition.

[3] The period of prosperity may, perhaps, be divided into three phases. In the first phase production is increased considerably as a result of fuller

principal element. The spirit of enterprise is paralyzed, particularly in the capital-producing industries, and from these it spreads by repercussion, causing general depression.[1]

Mitchell's *Business Cycles* is accounted by Joseph Schumpeter to be the "greatest work since Juglar."[2] Mitchell conceives that a theory of the business cycle must be a "descriptive analysis of the cumulative changes by which one set of business conditions transforms itself into another set."[3] The processes of a nation's business life are unceasing. There is no beginning and no end. The cycle is not due to the influence of disturbing causes from the outside, but to processes which run regularly within the world of business itself.

Stocks of goods are gradually depleted as depression wears on, and finally retail shopkeepers are compelled to place fresh orders with wholesale merchants, and these in turn with manufacturers. There thus develops an increase in the physical volume of business, and this

use of existing equipment and larger employment of labor. In the second phase more equipment is being built, but there is not much increase in the production of finished products. In the third phase, which runs off into the crisis, the new equipment adds to the total output of finished goods. Compare with Spiethoff's analysis discussed in Chapter IV, p. 68, of this book.

[1] Lescure, op. cit. pp. 413–414.

[2] Schumpeter, op. cit. p. 6. The importance of Mitchell's work is missed when one attempts to summarize his position, for its significance lies in the method of attack on the problem and the enormous amount of statistical information which it presents with respect to every phase of the cycle.

[3] W. C. Mitchell, *Business Cycles*, p. 449. University of California Press.

revival, once started, spreads rapidly over a large part
or even the whole of the field of business. Employment
is increased. Larger earnings for wageworkers and
higher profits for proprietors enable both classes to pay
such debts as may have accumulated during depression
and to enlarge their current purchases. Better and more
food is purchased; the demands for clothing, furniture,
amusements, and luxuries of all kinds are increased.
But for a time prices do not rise, partly because business
enterprises are still anxiously soliciting orders, and
partly because larger output means lower total unit cost
because of unused capacity. But the further expansion
of the physical volume of business eventually reaches
the point at which larger output means an increase in
prime costs and finally in supplementary costs.[1] Additional orders require overtime work, the hiring of new
and less efficient hands, the starting of old-fashioned
machines, and the installation of new equipment. With
higher costs, higher prices are asked when new orders
come in. A moderate increase in price quotations, if
thought to be an earnest of further future increases,
powerfully stimulates the volume of orders, and so
prices will rise still more. But wages lag behind prices.
Ideas of "just price" impede the free working of supply
and demand in the labor market. This lag affects the
margin of profits.[2]

[1] See also Alvin H. Hansen, "Prime Costs in the Business Cycle,"
Journal of Political Economy, February, 1924.

[2] W. C. Mitchell, op. cit. pp. 453–466.

But the rapid expansion of the industrial output breeds stresses. As soon as new industrial equipment is finished and put into active service, the demand for labor and raw materials is increased, and so prime costs rise sharply. At the same time the new equipment begins to pour out their products, and this tends to obstruct the advance of selling prices. Thus forces are set in motion which on the one hand tend to raise costs and on the other tend to check the advance of selling prices. Not only do prime costs rise, but also supplementary costs. High prices and high interest rates increase the cost of construction. Thus prosperity breeds an increase in the cost of doing business which threatens to diminish profits.[1]

Why cannot business men defend their margin of profits by marking up their selling prices sufficiently? Why cannot selling prices continue to rise indefinitely? The first answer is that the advance of the price level would ultimately be checked by the inadequacy of the quantity of money. But other causes generally check the rise in prices before this point is reached.[2] Public

[1] Mitchell, op. cit. pp. 472–489.

[2] Allyn A. Young gives a forceful argument on this point in his article "The Trend of Prices": "But the fact is, as we know, that no increase of the currency, no increase of credit, will push business and industry up with it beyond a certain point. Resistance or drag grows at an increasing rate." In this connection he discusses the relative inelasticity of supply of labor and materials, the growing inefficiency of labor and management, the overtaxed capacity of fixed equipment, notably the railroads. Declining efficiency and higher interest rates curtail the demand for constructional work. Moreover, as prosperity develops, the *distribution* of incomes changes; there is a shift in the *incidence* of demand. Cf. *American Economic Review*, Supplement, March, 1923.

utility rates are regulated by law; custom controls
the prices of many commodities, such as trade-marked
goods, newspapers, etc.; and many contracts are in
force to deliver goods according to specification at stipulated prices. Certain markets become overstocked
with goods; large stocks endanger the price situation.[1]
Finally, the rise in the interest rate checks (1) the
demand for constructional work (and this in turn
checks the demand for a vast variety of goods) and
(2) the piling up of large stocks for speculative purposes, since the heavy interest cost of carrying unsold
stocks saps the financial strength of even the largest
enterprises.[2]

When profit margins are threatened by the encroachment of costs, when these encroachments cannot be offset
by further advances of selling prices, and when the rate
at which profits are capitalized is reduced by the rise of
interest, then creditors begin to take alarm and press for
the settlement of their claims.[3]

Many plants close with the first shock of the crisis,
but reopen shortly to supply old orders and work up
inventories of raw materials. When this work is completed, output is further restricted. Workmen are dis-
charged, and this causes a decline in consumers' demand.

[1] See also G. E. Putnam, "Paper Profit and Business Cycles," *Harvard Business Review*, January, 1926, and F. Schmidt, "Die Industriekon-junktur — ein Rechenfehler!" in *Zeitschrift für Betriebswirtschaft*, 2. Sonderheft, 1927.

[2] Mitchell, op. cit. pp. 496–502.

[3] Ibid. p. 512.

The goods consumed are less varied and abundant; clothing and furniture are used longer and replaced when necessary by cheaper goods. Fuel and light are economized.[1] Prices decline, and costs are gradually reduced.

Money factors accelerate the readjustment of costs to selling prices, and so help to restore the prospects of profits. The accumulation of cash reserves increases the competition among banks for business and so helps to reduce discount rates. These factors are, however, not sufficient in themselves to produce the expansion of loans and deposits. But they contribute to the result. An increase in gold production tends to cut short and to mitigate periods of depression as well as to prolong and intensify periods of prosperity.[2]

Finally, the accumulated stocks of goods carried over from the period of prosperity are gradually disposed of. Consumers' demand during depression remains well above the fresh output of goods. Purchases exceed current income, for accumulated savings and personal credit at retail stores are drawn upon. Population grows apace. So the accumulated stocks are used up. New tastes are developed, and new types of goods put on the market. Retailers' purchases are increased, and this process reaches back to the wholesalers and manufacturers. Finally, new construction sets in. So depression at last breeds a revival of prosperity.

[1] Mitchell, op. cit. pp. 555–556.
[2] Ibid. pp. 561–562.

We have noted the tendency of costs to creep up on selling prices, and the reasons assigned for this fact by Veblen, Lescure, and Mitchell. To this analysis the present writer wishes to add a point, which was suggested to him by a statement made by Foster and Catchings in *Profits*.[1] As is well known, the advance in prices during the period of prosperity is made possible by the increased money purchasing power which is made available by the banks. This purchasing power is lent to business men, and they expend it on productive factors in an effort to expand their output of goods. But in a competitive society the *effort* to expand output may not actually succeed: it may simply result in bidding the factors away from other entrepreneurs. After the unemployed labor reserve has been absorbed, little or no additional labor can be got, and the supply of raw materials beyond a certain point is highly inelastic. As is well known a point is soon reached in the prosperity phase of the cycle beyond which production cannot be expanded appreciably because of limitation of supply of productive factors. The increased money outlay merely results in increasing the *prices paid* to the productive factors without increasing the supply of consumers' goods. "Money paid out in the expenses of production comes back in the form of consumers' demand for

[1] The statement in *Profits* is as follows: "The goods must be sold to consumers for more money than the expansion has provided" (p. 409). The argument presented by the writer is, however, fundamentally different from that of Foster and Catchings, and arrives, as we shall see later, at radically different conclusions.

goods." [1] With consumer demand increasing without
any corresponding increase in consumer supply, prices
will rise. But the advance in prices will not be as great
as the rise in expenses or money outlay, owing to the
fact that the expense item constitutes only a portion of
the total of the community's income. The factors
employed by business firms at stipulated rates do not
receive the total income, as a part is received by the
proprietors themselves. If, by way of illustration, the
employed factors receive 80 per cent of the national
income, and the proprietors receive 20 per cent, it is
clear that a 10 per cent increase in the rates paid to the
employed factors will result in only an 8 per cent increase
in the national income. On this basis, after a certain
point is reached in the prosperity phase of the cycle,
costs are bound to rise more rapidly than the total
money income, and so costs will gradually encroach
upon prices, and the profit margin will be narrowed.

[1] A. A. Young, *American Economic Review*, Supplement, 1923, p. 9.
In this statement by Professor Young there is implicit an analysis precisely similar to the one here made. See also Emil Lederer, "Konjunktur und Krisen," *Grundriss der Sozialökonomik*, IV, i (1925), pp. 361, 376–
404, and W. C. Mitchell's discussion of Lederer's views in *Business
Cycles: The Problem and its Setting* (1927), pp. 36–37.

CHAPTER VII

A CRITICAL ANALYSIS OF *PROFITS* IN THE LIGHT OF BUSINESS–CYCLE THEORIES

It is our purpose in this chapter to evaluate the leading conclusions of *Profits*[1] in the light of the theories discussed in the previous chapters. It shall be our purpose to point out similarities and contrasts, agreements and disagreements. In this manner we shall be able to judge more accurately the place that *Profits* occupies in the literature of the business cycle.

The authors of *Profits* contend that progress toward greater production is retarded because consumer buying does not keep pace with production. And one of the reasons which they give for this situation is that corporations and individuals must save. The savings of corporations and individuals are not used to purchase the goods already in the markets, but to bring about the production of more goods. They admit in their illustrative cases that in the process of expending these savings in the productive process the funds so spent are turned over to wage-earners and other producers, who use these funds, largely, to buy consumption goods. But at all events the result of the saving process is to

---

[1] By W. T. Foster and Waddill Catchings. See analysis of *Profits* in Chapter III of this book.

increase eventually the output of goods. Saving implies capital accumulation, and an increase in capital facilities implies an increase in the productive capacity of the nation and so an increase in the total output of goods. This is, of course, fully recognized in economic theory. Now the increased output of goods may not be matched with a corresponding increase in consumer money income, and so the extra output must either remain unsold or else be sold at lower prices. Other things remaining equal, saving tends essentially to depress prices, because of the increased productivity that follows from increased capital accumulation. And falling prices bring depression. This is the "dilemma of thrift," as Foster and Catchings put it. What is the remedy?

"Unproductive" expenditures applied at the proper time are useful, the authors tell us, as a remedy for depression. In this they are quite in agreement with Lauderdale, Malthus, and Hobson. "Unproductive" expenditures utilize money to take goods off the market instead of using it to place goods on the market. Even wasteful expenditure is defended as useful at certain times.[1]

This view is closely similar to that of Veblen. The increased productivity of modern industry, Veblen says, brings falling prices and depression. With Veblen this increased productivity is caused by the increasing efficiency of modern machine industry due to inventions and capital accumulations.

[1] *Profits*, pp. 403–404.

Veblen states plainly[1] that the position occupied by
Lauderdale, Malthus, Hobson, and others with respect
to wasteful expenditures is well taken. But the defense
of waste which they offered was incomplete. Waste,
Veblen says, seems necessary to keep trade brisk and
therefore to keep the industrial processes working at
their full capacity. The reason for this state of affairs
is the fact that the decisive ground which determines
the margin of activity in business and therefore in industry is the business men's reluctance to accept a reduction of profits *as measured in terms of price*. Now the
efficiency of the modern machine industry is so great
that the supply of goods and services is constantly outrunning the effective supply of the precious metals, and
so prices tend to fall. It is true that the growing efficiency of industry also increases the supply of the precious metals, and this increase has an effect on prices
contrary to that exerted by the increasing supply of
goods. The increased supply of precious metals acts to
correct or mitigate the trend of business toward chronic
depressions. Thus, while an increased supply of precious
metals is one of the least useful forms of wealth from
the standpoint of material serviceability, yet from the
standpoint of business prosperity at large it is probably
the most serviceable addition that can be made to
wealth. Rapidly increasing efficiency in the production
of other forms of wealth is detrimental to the business
interests, in that it brings falling prices and depression;

[1] Veblen, *The Theory of Business Enterprise*, p. 253.

but a rapid increase of the precious metals stimulates industrial activity, for it puts off depression by keeping up prices. But improvements in the industrial processes affect the cost of production of the precious metals in a less degree than the cost of other goods.[1] Moreover, the annual product of the money metals is a small fraction of the aggregate supply. The lower cost of the annual supply has therefore but a relatively slight effect upon the aggregate value of the total supply. But the case is different with consumers' and producers' goods. In the case of producers' goods, in particular, says Veblen, the annual output counts for by far the greater factor in making the current value of the available supply, if indeed it is not the only factor. Accordingly, it is only under very exceptional circumstances, at times when the precious metals are supplied with extraordinary freedom, that the increased output of those metals can offset the trend of business toward depression.[2]

To eliminate depression, therefore, it is necessary to stabilize the price level. But how? Veblen tackles this problem from the goods side of the equation of exchange rather than from the money side. His plan for stabilization calls for a reduction in the output of goods.[3] This may be accomplished by one of two ways: (1) by an

[1] This may or may not be true. Veblen did not take sufficient account of new discoveries of gold or of increasing banking efficiency.

[2] Veblen, op. cit. pp. 235–237.

[3] But no reasonable person will be able to follow Veblen in this proposal. The remedy is worse than the disease. It seeks to negative all progress.

increased unproductive consumption of goods and (2) by
the elimination of competition.

If enough of the national income is directed toward
wasteful expenditures, so as to admit of but a relatively
slight aggregate saving, the capital supply will be curtailed, production will be diminished because of the
restricted supply of one important factor of production, and so profitable prices can be maintained. If the
waste is sufficiently large, the current investment in
additional industrial equipment will not be sufficient to
lower prices appreciably through competition.[1]

As a matter of fact, however, Veblen does not believe
that "private initiative" is capable of carrying the
waste of goods to the point required. Saving is too in-
grained in the habits of modern business men to permit
a sufficient retardation of saving. Governments are
more "effective wasters." Witness the waste of war and
armaments, court and diplomatic establishments, etc.
But even the extraordinary public waste is altogether
inadequate to offset the surplus productivity of the
machine industry.[2] Possibly if the national income were
more equally distributed, "wasteful consumption"
would prove more nearly adequate. But, even so, the
balance cannot be maintained by wasteful consumption.
It must be maintained by curtailing and regulating the
output of goods.

Secure monopoly, then, is the remedy according to
Veblen.[3] Business coalition offsets industrial improve-

[1] Veblen, op. cit. p. 255   [2] Ibid. p. 257.   [3] Ibid. p. 258.

ments in so far as these improvements affect the cost of
goods more than they affect the value of the money
metals. Its effect is to neutralize the cheapening of
goods and services effected by current industrial progress by controlling output and thus maintaining prices.[1]
Thus in a community organized on the price system a
"salutary use of sabotage" — obstruction of industry
and such restrictions of output as will maintain prices
at a profitable level — is necessary to ward off depression. In no such community can the industrial system
be allowed to work at full capacity for any appreciable
interval of time. In order to adjust production to the
needs of the market (which needs are measured in
pecuniary terms), and so maintain a stable price level,
there must always be a certain variable margin of unemployment of plant and man power.[2]

To what extent, then, does Veblen agree with Foster
and Catchings? All agree that depression may follow
from excessive saving. All agree that "unproductive"
expenditure may effectively remedy depression. Veblen
holds that oversaving produces depression because it
results in an excessive supply of goods compared with
the available supply of money. In so far as the money
supply is being added to, this tendency is counteracted.
Foster and Catchings apparently hold that although the
output of gold mines may in part help to offset the

[1] Veblen, op. cit. p. 242.
[2] Thorstein B. Veblen, *The Engineers and the Price System*, pp. 8–9.
B. W. Huebsch.

deficiency of purchasing power, yet it is not at all adequate for this purpose.[1] The gold output, it is true,
increases consumer demand, since it puts purchasing
power into the hands of the gold producers and, in
large part, is used to buy consumers' goods without
being used first in the production of consumers' goods.
But this effect of gold production is comparatively in-
significant. The real effect of an increased output of
gold operates through the increase of bank reserves and
the consequent expansion of bank credit. But such
expansion is mainly for the purpose of facilitating the
production of goods, and therefore eventually results
(so Foster and Catchings believe) in a surplus of consumer supply over consumer demand. Thus Foster and
Catchings are even less optimistic than Veblen with
respect to the possibility of gold production's offsetting
the depressional tendency of the saving process. When
money is saved, it is used twice to bring goods to market
before it is used to take goods off the market. The
equilibrium of the supply of consumers' goods and the
volume of "money" offered for these goods is thus disturbed, unless something is done to offset the deficiency
of money demand caused by the saving process; and
this, they hold, is impossible as industry is now financed,
even in a society enjoying a rapid production of gold.
With Veblen it is not saving as such, but *oversaving*,
which results in a production of goods in excess of the
quantity that can be circulated by the existing quantity

[1] *Profits*, p. 352; see also Hastings, *Costs and Profits*, pp. 126–127.

of money at the prevailing price level. The overproduction runs in terms of the money economy. But Veblen recognizes that other factors besides "oversaving" may produce the surplus of goods in relation to the supply of money. Particularly, in this connection, does he emphasize inventions and improvements. These, to be sure, generally require more capital and saving, but not always.

Veblen, as we have noted, agrees with the Malthus-Hobson school that a more equal distribution of wealth and income would help to remedy the situation. But only to a limited extent, and only in so far as it would tend to limit capital accumulation, thus restricting production and checking the tendency to a fall in prices. Foster and Catchings, likewise, are skeptical of the efficacy of a more equal distribution of the products of industry as a remedy for depression, though a better distribution would tend to *delay* the deficiency of consumer buying which brings every period of prosperity to an end. A wider distribution of the ownership of securities helps to steady the flow of money into consumers' markets, since it tends to increase spending and reduce saving. "If, for example, there were only five million stockholders, a larger part of the dividends would be saved, and a smaller proportion spent, than would be the case if there were ten million owners."[1] Yet greater equality of income, while it might somewhat diminish voluntary saving, cannot solve the problem,

[1] *Profits*, pp. 354–357.

for, the authors tell us, corporations and individuals must, in self-defense, necessarily save.

Foster and Catchings see no hope of eliminating saving and so increased production; nor, in fact, do they wish to do so. And the adjustment of the "money" supply to production, with a view to stabilizing prices, also appears hopeless. The deficiency of demand created by saving and increased production cannot, they say, be offset by an expansion of the volume of money. For "money is expended mainly to facilitate the production of goods; and the goods must be sold to consumers for more money than the expansion has provided."[1] Instead of the expansion of money counteracting the effect of saving and increased production, it operates eventually to reënforce the disturbing influence of the saving process. And the reason for this anomalous state of affairs is that an expansion of the volume of "money" develops a greater expansion of production than of consumer purchasing power.

At first, indeed, the expansion of the volume of "money" appears to serve as a satisfactory counteracting force against the tendency of saving to depress prices. But only for a time. In the end it makes matters worse. For a time the expansion of the volume of "money" increases the consumers' incomes without increasing the supply of consumers' goods. Production in the modern economy takes time. But finally, unless the expansion of the volume of money continues at an

[1] Ibid. chap. xxxi.

increasing *rate*, the increased output of goods exceeds the addition to consumer purchasing power and so prices will fall. Thus, the authors contend, the final effect of an expansion of the volume of money is to create a further deficiency in consumers' demand. This is the second main reason which, it is charged, accounts for the failure of consumer buying to keep pace with production.

The points made by the authors of *Profits* may, then, be summarized as follows:

1. That saving, by increasing production,[1] tends to depress prices.[2] This follows from the failure of consumers' money demand to keep pace with the increased production of goods.

2. That the first effect of an expansion of the volume of "money" is to raise prices, for production takes time, and so the money incomes of consumers (paid out while production is in process) are increased before the new goods can be put on the market.

3. That the output of consumers' goods must eventually outrun the expansion of consumers' incomes, for

---

[1] And also in part by the lengthening of the circuit time from consumption to consumption; that is, by retarding the circuit flow of money.

[2] Foster and Catchings, however, do not sufficiently recognize the considerable margin of flexibility in the industrial system. Within limits it is quite possible for business to adjust itself to a slowly falling price level without serious consequences. This is particularly true if it is possible for business men to meet the price decline with cost-reducing improvements and the elimination of waste. Recent experiences in the United States indicate that it is quite possible to maintain a high level of production and profits in spite of a slowly sagging price level.

each expansion furnishes consumers with only enough
money to buy the additional goods at cost. Unless, then,
this is offset by a further expansion of the volume of
money at an increasing rate, the final effect is to depress
prices.[1]

4. That the disturbance of economic equilibrium
caused by saving can therefore not be counteracted by
an appropriate adjustment of the volume of "money."

The doctrine of Foster and Catchings reduced to its
lowest terms comes to this: The equilibrium of consumer demand and supply is upset by (1) saving and
(2) by the expansion of the volume of "money." But
saving is necessary in a progressive society. Furthermore, saving implies an increased output of goods, and
this necessitates an increase in the volume of money
or circulating media, else there will be a fall in prices.
Hence society is caught in a trap. It cannot stand still;
and yet if it goes forward, it is faced with this inevitable
disruption of the economic equilibrium. This is the
dilemma, as Foster and Catchings see it. What is the
solution?

Let us consider the conclusions of Foster and Catchings in the light of the theories which we have discussed
in the preceding chapters. It is well recognized in
economic literature, as we have seen, that the business

[1] Cf. the criticism by N. Shaposhnikoff in *The Problems of Economic
Conditions* (The Conjuncture Institute, Moscow), Vol. III, Issue I
(1927), p. 155. He remarks that the means of understanding the nature
of economic cycles does not rest with the conduct of those who spend
money but with that of those (namely, the banks) who create it.

cycle is a function of a dynamic society. But saving is only one aspect of a dynamic society. In this respect the economists go further than Foster and Catchings. From the time of the classical economists it has been well recognized that the three great factors of economic dynamics are (1) inventions, discoveries, and improvements, (2) capital accumulations, and (3) increase in population. Foster and Catchings take account of only one of them. They have, in fact, omitted the leading factors of economic dynamics — inventions, discoveries, and improvements. As we have seen, it is well established by Spiethoff, Cassel, Robertson, Pigou, and Schumpeter that these factors are constantly upsetting the economic equilibrium. Moreover, these economists have analyzed the relation of inventions and discoveries to the production and accumulation of capital goods. This Foster and Catchings have not done. They merely state that corporations and individuals must save.

With respect to capital accumulation we have seen that it is well recognized in economic literature that while the new capital goods are being made, consumer demand is likely to outrun consumer supply. The reason is twofold: (1) the production of new capital goods is likely to take place under conditions that invoke an increase in bank credit; (2) while the capital goods are being produced and the money income of the community is being increased, the output of consumers' goods is not increased until the capital goods have been completed. The first of these points has been firmly established, as we have seen, by Robertson, Pigou, Cassel, Wicksell, Fisher, and Hawtrey; the second, notably, by Carver, Aftalion, and J. M. Clark. That this unstable situation inevitably works a reaction we have seen in the researches of Veblen, Lescure, and W. C. Mitchell.

Now saving may conceivably be accomplished at (1) a uniform rate of increase or (2) an irregular, fluctuating rate of increase. Whether saving is uniform and steady or is concentrated in certain periods, thus going on by spurts, makes a large difference. Does saving per se necessarily disrupt the economic equilibrium, or is it only intermittent, irregular saving that disrupts the equilibrium? Is it possible to counteract these disrupting tendencies and maintain substantial equilibrium?

The saving process may, moreover, be effected by either of two methods: (1) voluntary saving and (2) compulsory saving. The degree to which the economic equilibrium is disturbed is determined in large part by the *means* by which the saving is accomplished.

Foster and Catchings do not appear to see that it makes any difference whether the saving is *steady* or *intermittent*. For them saving as such is a disrupting factor regardless of the conditions of the rate of increase. Nor is it clear that they see that the *method* by which the saving function is carried out is significant. To these questions we shall now turn our attention.

C. F. Bickerdike advances the view that a "smooth state of growth, with a uniform price level, is possible if two conditions are fulfilled: (1) growth is uniform,

(2) saving and the creation of bank credit always continually equal the amount required for financing growth. . . . If these conditions are not fulfilled there is almost inevitably involved not only disturbance of individual prices, but disturbance of the general level of prices, and, under ordinary conditions of individualism, oscillations of trade activity." [1]

But, remarks Bickerdike, the "maintenance of a uniform price level with growth is possible only if money is increased at the same uniform rate. The mere fact of saving does not provide the growth of money." [2]

This presents precisely the issue raised by Foster and Catchings. Contrary to the view of Bickerdike they deny that the increase in money is alone sufficient to yield a stabilized price level. Any expansion in the value of money is itself a disturbing factor, upsetting the economic equilibrium and resulting in price fluctuations. For a time it acts as a force counteracting the tendency toward a fall in prices caused by growth or by saving, but eventually it produces, on its own account, a fall in prices thus reënforcing the original downward tendency.

It is important to inquire into the merits of this argument. With a uniform rate of saving and a consequent growth of production, is it possible to maintain a stable price level? Foster and Catchings say No. It is safe to say that the weight of economic opinion is against them.

[1] *The Economic Journal*, September, 1924, p. 422.
[2] Ibid. p. 421.

It is admitted that saving, other things remaining equal, tends to depress prices.[1] If, however, at this juncture the discount rate is lowered, the effect will be to counteract the downward tendency.[2] If the discount rate is reduced below the rate of profit in industry, the effect will be to stimulate borrowing on the part of business men, as shown by Thornton, Ricardo, Juglar, Sidgwick, Giffen, Wicksell, Marshall, Fisher, and Hawtrey.[3] The expansion of bank loans increases the money purchasing power of business men, and prices tend to rise, thus counteracting the tendency toward a depression of prices. Robertson puts it as follows: "If the bank takes no action there will be a fall in the price level and an increase in the real value of the public's money stock. . . . By making additional loans of an appropriate amount, at an appropriate pace, the bank can counteract the fall in the price level."[4]

[1] Cf. the following from Bickerdike: ". . . we should find that whilst the saving was being made, the price level would be reduced below what it would otherwise have been, and when, at a later time, the saver spent the interest, or both the interest and the capital, the price level would be raised. The rest of the community would get more real return for their money during the time of saving and would get less at a later time." — *Economic Journal*, September, 1924, p. 420

[2] Increased production may be financed out of savings or out of bank credit. If financed by the former method, prices will tend to fall; if by the latter, prices will tend to rise. If too little saving and too much bank credit is used, prices will rise. But this can be stopped by raising the discount rate. This action will check the issue of bank credit and stimulate voluntary saving. If prices are falling, the discount rate may be lowered, and opposite reactions will follow.

[3] Cf. Chapter VI, pp. 132–149, of this book.

[4] *Banking Policy and the Price Level*, p. 54. P. S. King & Son.

The effect of the action of the bank, therefore, is to permit an increase in production without lowering the price level.

So far Foster and Catchings would probably agree. But, they would say, let us follow out the matter further. Let us see what is the ultimate effect of an expansion of bank credit. The first effect of this expansion is to put more money into the hands of consumers. While the additional capital goods are being made, and so long as no additional consumers' goods are being placed on the market, the tendency is to offset the depression in prices caused by the increased production consequent upon the past accumulation of capital goods. But the enforced saving eventually brings forth a new batch of capital goods, and when these begin to function the production of consumables is still further increased, and so prices will again tend to fall unless the volume of bank loans is again expanded. And if the tendency for prices to fall is to be checked, then expansion of back credit must, they tell us, continue at an increasing *rate*. The reason given is that the expanded volume of money is paid out in expenses of production. Consumers' money incomes are therefore increased, as a result of the expansion, by an amount equal only to the expenses of producing the additional goods. Therefore when the finished goods are finally placed on the market they are confronted with a purchasing power in the hands of the consumers which is equivalent only to the cost of producing those goods. In the long run, therefore, prices must fall.

The essential fallacy in this argument is that it assumes that every expansion of productive expenditures
(consequent upon an increase in the volume of "money")
will result in a nearly corresponding increase in the
physical volume of production. But, as a matter of fact,
such is not the case. As is well known, in the period of
revival and during the first phase of prosperity, increased
outlays for materials and wages do result in an increase
in physical production. This follows from the more complete utilization of existing fixed capital and equipment
and a larger employment of labor. In the second phase
of prosperity, production is not materially increased, the
reason being that the productive forces of the community are already fully utilized. But the expansion of
bank credit may continue. The additional purchasing
power placed in the hands of business men is now used
not to buy *more* factors of production (for more are,
within limits, not available), but to bid factors away
from their competitors. The *expenses* of production rise,
but not production.[1] Under these circumstances it is
clear that an expansion of the volume of "money,"
however slight, would tend to raise prices. Therefore it
is not true that the expansion must proceed at an accelerating rate. What is true, indeed, is that an expansion of the volume of "money" will eventually raise the
expenses of production more than it will raise prices.[2]
The competitive bidding for productive factors conse-

[1] Cf. O. M. W. Sprague, in *American Economic Review*, March, 1921.
[2] See Chapter VI, pp. 159–160, of this book.

quent upon the expansion of bank loans results in the
distribution of a larger proportion of the national income
among the *employed* factors, leaving a smaller proportion for the proprietors. Wages would rise and business
profits would fall. But this does not mean that the price
level cannot be stabilized by an intelligent discount
policy. It does mean, however, a tendency toward a
narrowing of the profit margin.[1] But this tendency in
a dynamic society is constantly being counteracted by
improved processes of production which lower costs and
raise the margin of profit. These factors Foster and
Catchings have not adequately taken account of. If,
however, in spite of these cost-reducing forces the margin of profit continues to fall, this fact does not imply
a consequent fall in the price level, but rather a falling
off in the volume of saving. Our conclusion, then, is
that it is theoretically quite possible through an intelligent discount policy to offset any downward tendency
in prices.[2]

[1] Cf. the answer of James Mill to Malthus in his *Elements of Political
Economy*, p. 242. See also J. S. Mill, *Principles of Political Economy*
(Ashley's edition), p. 68, and F. W. Taussig, *Principles of Economics*,
Vol. II, p. 57.

[2] Cf. J. R. Bellerby, *The Control of Credit*. There are, however, many
practical difficulties which in the present state of society may prove in-
superable. Moreover, it should be noted that many economists who
support a regulated discount policy nevertheless refuse to accept the view
that the business cycle is a purely monetary phenomenon. See Joseph
Schumpeter, "Kreditkontrolle," *Archiv für Sozialwissenschaft und Sozialpolitik*, 1925; A. C. Pigou, in *Is Unemployment Inevitable?* T. E. Gregory,
in *American Economic Review*, March, 1925; and W. C. Mitchell, in
American Economic Review, Supplement, 1922.

Consider, however, a condition in which the rate of saving is irregular, being concentrated in certain periods. This is the situation in the world as it actually is. Saving proceeds by spurts. Inventions, discoveries, and improvements raise the prospective rate of profit and stimulate saving. Moreover, the voluntary saving thus engendered is almost certain to be supplemented in an unregulated money economy by the enforced saving imposed on the general public by an extension of credit.[1]

Now it is held by Spiethoff, Cassel, and Bickerdike that such irregular growth and sporadic saving is not consistent with stabilization of business and industry. Cassel, it will be remembered, contends that the business cycle essentially consists of an irregular production of fixed capital. Business stability requires a fairly uniform rate of growth and capital accumulation. Perfect stability cannot be achieved in a dynamic society which experiences a continued fluctuation in the prospective profit rate because of inventions, discoveries, and improvements; but the fluctuations can be greatly mitigated by a stabilized price level.

Let us assume that a new discovery raises the general rate of profit in industry. Saving is stimulated thereby. There is a tendency to borrow heavily from banks. Capital will be produced in large volume. If industry were allowed to run its unregulated course the inevitable result would be a period of intense prosperity followed

---

[1] Cf. Chapter IV, pp. 87–97, of this book.

by a period of depression. But now suppose the high prospective profit rate is balanced by a high rate of discount with a view to stabilizing prices.[1] This action will check the expansion of bank credit, prevent the rise in prices, and thus forestall any enforced saving. The high rate of interest will, however, stimulate a large volume of voluntary saving. Consider the following from Pigou:

Under a system of stabilized prices when business men wanted more real resources to invest in setting labor to work, they could only get them by offering a higher rate of real interest so as to induce the owners of fixed incomes voluntarily to surrender a part of them. They would obtain the extra cash they wanted in order to pay their workpeople in return for promises to lenders, and there would be no further reaction of any sort. To put the same thing otherwise: prices would not change, but the workpeople would have money to spend which the owner of fixed incomes would otherwise have spent, and this change in the distribution of spending power would be the only change.[2]

Stabilization of the price level therefore involves the elimination of the bulk of enforced saving. This is the price that the community must pay for stabilization.

If the banking and monetary arrangement are so altered that prices are kept stable when the demand for new capital

[1] Cf. Georg Halm, who says that "without the difference in the height of the profit rate and interest rate the conjuncture movement would not even come into being." — *Jahrbücher für Nationalökonomie und Statistik,* August, 1926

[2] *Is Unemployment Inevitable?* (pp. 101–102).

rises, there will be no forced levy. Consequently, the supply of capital will be smaller, and the rate of interest required to balance demand and supply will be higher than it is when there is a forced levy.[1]

It was not purely by normal savings that the rapid growth of savings in England and America during the nineteenth century, in Germany from 1870 to 1914, was financed, but largely by extension of bank credit in excess, for the time being, of normal saving, resulting in periodical inflations.[2]

The capital accumulation of the past has been fostered not merely by the unequal distribution of wealth and income, but also by price fluctuations. Stabilization implies a possible slowing down of at least one factor of progress; namely, capital accumulation.

However, it is perhaps ample compensation that the elimination of enforced saving would dispose of the worst features of industrial fluctuations. The economic equilibrium is disturbed by the constant temptation and desire to obtain the necessary capital without the arduous process of saving. The equilibrium is disrupted, partly because we try to have our cake and eat it too; we try to accumulate capital without saving. The thing cannot be done. The effort to do so pumps into the economic system the intoxicating virus of inflation. The disease runs its course. Stresses and strains develop, and the collapse finally comes.

[1] Pigou, op. cit. p. 111.
[2] C. F. Bickerdike, *Economic Journal*, September, 1925, p. 378.

Moreover, the stabilization of prices would tend to minimize speculative buying for stock. And, this, as we have seen in Chapter V, is a vitally important factor in existing business fluctuations.

While most of the economists cited have more or less faith in the mitigating influence of a stabilized price level, nevertheless many have little hope of eliminating the business cycle so long as we have a dynamic society. Foster and Catchings find the cause of the business cycle essentially in the saving process. But saving is only one aspect of a dynamic society. Spiethoff, Schumpeter, Fisher, Cassel, Pigou, and Robertson, among many others, particularly emphasize, as we have seen, inventions, scientific discoveries, new resources, new processes, new products, as factors disturbing the economic equilibrium. These forces have within them explosive elements tending to disrupt the economic equilibrium. So long as revolutions in technology are thrust upon the industrial system, so long as there are undeveloped resources to exploit, the hope of a completely stabilized economic order is small. This view of the fundamental causes of the cycle is much broader than that given by Foster and Catchings. The more complex the underlying forces, the more difficult the problem of stabilization. In this respect Foster and Catchings may be said to have greater faith than many economists, perhaps most, in finding a solution for the problem.

On the other hand, Foster and Catchings are more pessimistic with respect to the possibilities of an intelli-

gent discount policy than most of the economists cited.
Any increase of purchasing power by means of an expansion of credit (effected by manipulation of the discount rate) has, as they see it, in the final analysis a
disrupting rather than a stabilizing influence, *unless the
use made of the credit is also controlled.* While they do not
go into the problem of remedies in *Profits*, still it is
rather clear what the nature of their remedy would be.
When prices tend to fall they would encourage purchasing activity on the part of *consumers* by all possible
measures. One means of stimulating consumer purchasing would be to press forward public works and to
finance these out of additional bank loans.[1] This would
increase the total money purchasing power of the community, but the significant thing is the *manner in which
this additional purchasing power is used.* With respect to
this point Hawtrey takes a position squarely opposed
to that of Foster and Catchings. With Hawtrey it is
sufficient to strengthen the community's monetary purchasing power without directing in any way the use
made of this purchasing power. With him public works
are not significant in themselves: they are significant

[1] *Profits*, pp. 331, 340. Note especially the following: Deficiencies in
demand may sometimes be "partly offset or more than offset by increases in government expenditures which involve permanent increases
in the volume of money in circulation, whether the money comes from
banks or from printing presses. Indeed, it may be in this direction that
ultimately the solution of the problem of adequate consumer demand will
be found" (p. 340). In their earlier work on *Money* they suggested that
whenever prices began to fall the government should stimulate consumer
buying by buying securities in the open market (p. 361).

only in that they furnish an excuse for the expansion of credit and so increase the purchasing power of the community.[1] The same results could be accomplished without building public works. The expansion of credit is the really significant thing. With Foster and Catchings the expenditures of funds on public works is important because such expenditure strengthens consumer demand without adding more goods to the already overstocked markets. If, however, the additional credit were granted to business men it would be used to expand the production of current consumers' goods.

Hawtrey, among others, believes that business can be stabilized by controlling bank credit through the discount rate. It is not necessary to control the *use* made of this credit. Market price is a sufficient guide as to *what* shall be produced, whether long-time consumption goods, such as public libraries, museums, parks, etc., or current consumption goods or production goods. Foster and Catchings believe that it is necessary to direct the currents of consumption and production.

In so far as Foster and Catchings hold that the expansion of bank credit (without any control of the *use* made of the bank credit) is a disrupting rather than a stabilizing force, their position is not sound. In so far as they hold that the control of the *use* of the additional bank credit is a further stabilizing factor, their position is, as the present writer sees it, sound. The control of credit by means of the discount rate works more effec-

[1] Cf. *Economic Journal*, March, 1926, p. 98.

tively to check a boom than to stimulate purchasing in a depressed market. At such times it is necessary, as Bellerby puts it, to use "all possible measures adopted by State and banks"[1] to encourage purchasing activity. Nearly all the economists agree that state action along these lines would be helpful in a problem that is difficult enough at best. But to agree with this position does not imply acceptance of the view that an intelligent discount policy unaccompanied by any control of the *use* of credit is, in the final analysis, a disrupting rather than a stabilizing factor. And this, reduced to its lowest terms, is the position of Foster and Catchings.[2]

As an explanation of the business cycle *Profits* is weak in the following particulars:

1. It overlooks the disturbing influence of dynamic factors other than saving, notably inventions, scientific discoveries, new resources, new processes, and new products.

2. It fails to distinguish between the effect of the saving process per se and the effect of sporadic, irregular, and intermittent saving.

3. It takes no account of the *manner* in which saving may be accomplished, whether voluntary or enforced.

---

[1] J. R. Bellerby, *Monetary Stability*, pp. 25, 49–51. Macmillan and Company, Limited.

[2] It should be noted, however, that they admit that the control of bank credit through the discount rate is effective as a stabilizing force to check inflation (cf. *Money*, pp. 358–359). What is disrupting, in their view, is the *expansion* of bank credit unaccompanied by a control of the use of the credit.

Yet the method by which social savings are made is of the highest significance for an understanding of the business cycle.

4. It fails to take cognizance of the fact that an expansion of bank credit beyond a certain point raises costs and selling prices without increasing production appreciably. *Profits* therefore minimizes the ultimate counter-depressional influence of an expansion of bank credit.

5. It fails to recognize that the *ultimate*[1] tendency of an expansion of bank credit which does not increase at an accelerated rate is not a fall in prices (as contended in *Profits*) but a decline in the rate of profit. However, a gradual decline in the rate of profit is perfectly consistent with a stabilized economy. Moreover, *Profits* overlooks the cost-reducing factors which counteract the downward tendency of the rate of profit.

6. It discounts *price* as the guide to production and implies the necessity of regulating the uses made of newly created purchasing power.

7. It minimizes the efficacy of an intelligent discount policy as a stabilizing factor.

8. It overlooks, largely, the disturbing influence of the irregular accumulation of stocks and the significance, as a steadying factor, of the movement to stabilize inventories.

---

[1] The authors of *Profits*, see of course, that the *immediate* effect is to raise prices.

CHAPTER VIII

THE PRESENT STATUS OF BUSINESS-CYCLE THEORY

In the present stage of economic theory the business cycle is, in the opinion of many economists, an unsolved riddle.[1] Professor Adolph Löwe[2] of Kiel University, Germany, even doubts that the wealth of statistical material that has been poured out during the last ten or fifteen years has made any contributions toward the theoretical analysis of cyclical fluctuations. The fundamental opposing theories still stand, he thinks, unreconciled over against each other. There are still, as he sees it, three main systems. On the one hand the cycle is explained from the money side, and on the other from the goods side; and if from the goods side, the analysis proceeds either from the conditions of production or from the conditions of consumption.[3]

---

[1] Tougan-Baranowsky, in the preface to his *Les Crises industrielles en Angleterre* (1913), refers to the industrial cycle as the most enigmatical phenomenon in modern economic life and one which economic science has not yet solved.

[2] "Wie ist Konjunkturtheorie überhaupt möglich?" in *Weltwirtschaftliches Archiv*, October, 1926.

[3] It is interesting to note that Löwe suggests that these theories can be differentiated according to nations, the monetary theory being the ruling doctrine in the Anglo-Saxon economics, whereas the Continental conception continues to direct its view preponderantly on the goods side.

The present writer is less pessimistic with respect to the present status of business-cycle theory. Is it quite correct to say that the fundamental theories stand unreconciled over against each other? In the opinion of Professor W. C. Mitchell, while the literature on the business cycle is, indeed, highly controversial, nevertheless the differences among recent writers are mainly differences in the distribution of emphasis.[1] D. H. Robertson contends that "in the deathless words of the Dodo, everybody has won and all must have prizes, in the sense that almost all the writers who have made any serious contribution to the study of the matter appear to have had a considerable measure of right on their side."[2] Yet he admits that "there is as yet no single comprehensive explanation which may be said to hold the field." He is of the opinion that the "most important work which remains to be done lies in the direction of developing and synthesizing the various and often conflicting opinions which have been already expressed."[3]

Many writers have contributed to this synthesizing work during the last fifteen years or so. Most prominent among these are Fisher, Mitchell, Robertson, Pigou, and Cassel. Mitchell, indeed, sought to allay the conflict, in part, by making his theory of business cycles

[1] Wesley C. Mitchell, *Business Cycles and Unemployment*, p. 7. McGraw-Hill Book Company.

[2] D. H. Robertson, *A Study of Industrial Fluctuations*, p. 1. P. S. King & Son.

[3] Ibid. p. 2.

a "descriptive analysis" and, in part, by endeavoring to harmonize the opposing views.

By the year 1913 the status of business-cycle theory, to put the matter succinctly, was approximately as follows: The monetary theory, beginning with Thornton and culminating with Marshall (1888) and Wicksell (1897), had been specifically applied to the business cycle by Irving Fisher in his *Rate of Interest* in 1907, and by Hawtrey in his *Good and Bad Trade* in 1913. The old underconsumption theory was pretty generally discredited. Instead, Spiethoff in 1901 had placed *production* in the foreground. The business cycle, he held, consists in the fluctuations in the production of capital goods, and these fluctuations spring from the changes in the demand for fixed capital growing out of inventions, discoveries of new resources, and technical improvements. But the rôle played by consumers was not long without sponsors. In 1909 Aftalion, while granting the fluctuations in the production of fixed capital as characteristic of the business cycle, nevertheless maintained that the initiatory forces were to be found in changes in consumers' demand, which in turn produced much greater fluctuations in the production of fixed capital.

By 1913, then, the leading opposing theories were (1) the monetary theory of Wicksell and Hawtrey, (2) the capital-production theory of Spiethoff, (3) the fluctuating consumer-demand theory of Aftalion. At that point the opposing theories were indeed, for the most part, unreconciled.

Irving Fisher had, however, in his *Rate of Interest* in 1907 made a thorough analysis of the interrelations of inventions, discoveries, the rate of profit, the rate of interest, and the price level, thus synthesizing in effect the work of Wicksell and Spiethoff.

On the other hand, Mitchell's work in 1913 exerted a synthesizing influence chiefly by laying emphasis upon a descriptive analysis of the business cycle. This method made clear the interrelations of numerous factors which formerly had been viewed more or less in isolation.

The subsequent work of Robertson, Pigou, and Cassel helped to synthesize the theories of the productionists and the consumptionists. Robertson and Pigou placed special emphasis, however, upon the work of Aftalion, and Cassel's work appears to be particularly influenced by Spiethoff. So far as monetary factors are concerned, Pigou gives on the whole more weight to these than do Robertson and Cassel.

By 1913 the leading fundamental principles for a theory of the business cycle had been developed. Some work of first-rate theoretical importance, notably that of Bickerdike, J. M. Clark, and L. K. Frank, has been added since. Moreover progress has been made in coördinating and synthesizing these principles.

There are certain fundamental principles relating to the business cycle which are accepted by a very considerable number of writers representing various points of view. The leading principles referred to are as follows:

I. *The Mechanism of Expansion and Contraction.* The principle
   may be stated as follows : If for any reason the prospective
   profit rate deviates from the rate of interest charged in the
   loan market, the discrepancy between them tends to develop
   into an expansion or contraction of business, depending
   upon whether the profit rate is above or below the loan rate.
   This principle was developed and accepted by Thornton,
   Ricardo, Juglar, Giffen, Sidgwick, Marshall, Wicksell,
   Fisher, Hawtrey, Cassel, Hahn, Röpke, Pigou, and Allyn
   Young. Any one of the following factors may cause this
   discrepancy.

   1. New inventions, discovery of new resources, improved
      methods of production (Spiethoff, Schumpeter, Fisher,
      W. C. Mitchell, Cassel, Robertson, Pigou, Adams).
   2. Large crops [1] (Moore, Fisher, Veblen, Pigou, Robertson,
      Spiethoff).

---

[1] Large crops, as we have already shown, may affect the business
cycle in various ways. In so far as the influence operates by way of
low prices of raw materials (which low prices increase the prospective
rate of profit), the importance of crops is clearly small compared to
that of inventions, improvements, and the discovery of new resources.
These latter cause business men to look far ahead to great prospects
of profit-making which call for the building of large quantities of
fixed capital. The low prices of raw materials, due to a bountiful harvest, reduce costs and enhance the prospects of profit-making, to be
sure, but only for, say, a year ; no great vista of exploitation and expansion is opened up. Moreover, it should be noted that the other effects
of crop fluctuations — shifts in consumers' demand, changes in the
purchasing power of farmers and in the demands made upon transportation and storage facilities — are also limited to a relatively short
period. It is doubtful that business calculations with respect to crops
and their bearing upon prospects of profit-making extend beyond
a year or so. On the other hand, inventions and discoveries project
their influence far into the future. It therefore seems probable that the
effect of crop fluctuations upon the business cycle is small compared
to the large influence of inventions and discoveries as initiating forces
of prosperity.

3. Discovery of new gold mines, new methods of producing gold (Juglar, Sidgwick, Giffen, Marshall, Wicksell, Veblen, Fisher, Robertson, Spiethoff, Pigou).
4. Great Wars (Veblen, Robertson, Pigou, Fisher, Spiethoff, Adams).
5. New products (Schumpeter, Robertson, Pigou, Aftalion, W. C. Mitchell).
6. Shifts in consumers' demand (Aftalion, Allyn Young, Robertson, Pigou, Carver, Bickerdike, J. M. Clark).

It is to be noted that it is at this point that the monetary theory joins forces with the productionists and the consumptionists. The mechanism is essentially of a monetary character, but the initiatory forces operating upon that mechanism are independent variables impinging upon the monetary mechanism from the outside. These independent variables are changes in the arts, changes in consumers' demand, and changes in the bounties of nature.[1]

II. *The Cumulation of Expansion and Contraction.* This principle may be stated as follows: Once the economic equilibrium is broken, forces are let loose which tend to intensify the disruption of equilibrium. The factors reënforcing and intensifying the disruption of equilibrium are as follows:
1. The rise (or fall) in prices tends to widen the discrepancy between the profit rate and loan market rate because of the wider (or smaller) margin of profit consequent upon

[1] These factors operate to produce (or are expected to produce) lower costs in the industries affected. Large profits are anticipated. On the basis of these expectations business enterprises increase their capitalization and borrow more heavily from the banks. The ensuing expansion of bank credit results in an intensified competitive bidding for materials, equipment, and labor, and finally (through the ensuing rise of money incomes) for consumers' goods. Thus the price-level is forced upward.

the lag of costs behind selling prices (Veblen, Lescure, W. C. Mitchell, Hawtrey, Fisher, Wicksell, Cassel, Allyn Young, and Pigou).

2. Slight fluctuations in consumers' demand produce large fluctuations in the demand for semifinished products and raw materials because of the tendency to "stock up" in an upward-moving market and to sell from stock in a falling market (W. C. Mitchell, H. B. Hastings, L. K. Frank, T. W. Mitchell, F. W. Taussig, W. I. King, R. G. Hawtrey, J. M. Clark, and S. S. Kuznets).

The accompanying diagram, which is similar to that given by L. K. Frank,[1] illustrates the interrelations.

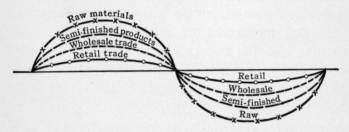

3. Slight fluctuations in consumers' demand produce large fluctuations in the demand for fixed capital (Carver, Aftalion, Bickerdike, J. M. Clark, W. C. Mitchell, Cassel, Robertson, Pigou).

This interrelation is illustrated in the following diagram, in which *B* is derived mathematically from *A*. The depreciation rate on fixed capital is presumed to be 10 per cent per annum. Accordingly a 5 per cent increase in consumer demand will give rise to a 50 per cent increase in the demand for fixed capital. From the

[1] *Quarterly Journal of Economics*, August, 1923.

diagram it will be noted that while the demand for consumers' goods (curve A) fluctuates within a range of thirty points, the demand for fixed capital (curve B) fluctuates within a range of one hundred points.

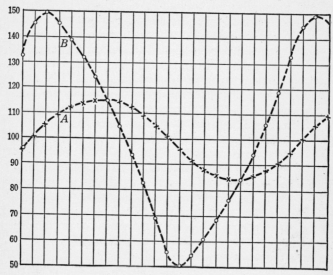

III. *The Self-Limitation of Expansion or Contraction.* This principle may be stated as follows: Eventually the cumulative reaction is checked, and the industrial mechanism is brought back toward equilibrium by limiting or restraining forces which automatically are brought into operation. The limiting or restraining forces are as follows:

1. The limited supply of the prime factors of production. The expansion is checked by the limited available supply of labor and raw materials, particularly agricultural raw materials (Spiethoff, Robertson, Cassel, Sombart, Veblen, Hull, Lescure, W. C. Mitchell, Allyn Young).

2. The law of proportionality. Industrial units which for
one reason or another cannot readily expand their
fixed plant soon face a condition of increasing cost in
terms of the variable factors and, eventually, conditions of increasing total-unit cost.[1] The limitation of
the fixed plant, utilized beyond the point of highest
economic efficiency, results in higher cost of production
per unit of output. This well-known law of proportionality has been applied to the business-cycle phenomenon by Alfred Marshall [2] and W. C. Mitchell.[3]

3. The limited supply of "capital disposal." There follows
an encroachment of the capital market upon the money
market, the rate of interest rises, and in consequence
a check is imposed, particularly upon the expansion of
retailers' stocks and the construction of fixed capital
(Tougan-Baranowsky, Spiethoff, Cassel, Halm, Robertson, Pigou, W. C. Mitchell, Hawtrey, and Taussig).

4. The lag of *percentage* increase in purchasing power (arising
out of bank loans made to producers) in relation to the
percentage increase in consumer supply and in cost of
production. The upward movement of prices is thus
checked (Foster and Catchings, Lederer).[4]

5. As the *rate of increase* of retail and consumer buying begins to decline (due to 3 and 4, above) the *absolute*
volume of demand for fixed capital declines. Thus the
demand for fixed capital begins to fall long before there
is an absolute decline in the absolute demand for consumers' goods (see diagram on page 194). As soon as
the capital-producing industries begin to decline, work-

---

[1] For an extended exposition of the effect of proportionality of factors
upon the business cycle see Alvin H. Hansen, "Prime Costs in the
Business Cycle," *Journal of Political Economy*, February, 1924.

[2] *Principles of Economics* (7th ed.), pp. 373–421.

[3] *Business Cycles*, p. 563.

[4] For a full treatment see Chapters VI and VII, pp. 159–160 and
176–178 of this book.

men in these fields become unemployed, and so consumer demand is slowed down still more. Thus the decline in the *rate of increase* of consumer buying brings about an absolute decline in the demand for fixed equipment, and curtailment here, in turn, forces a further decline in the rate of increase in consumer buying until eventually an absolute decline is brought about. (Bickerdike, J. M. Clark, Pigou, Cassel, and W. C. Mitchell.) [1]

The outline here given indicates a considerable measure of agreement with respect to (1) the disturbing forces, (2) the accelerating forces, and (3) the limiting forces which operate to produce business cycles.

There remains to consider the question as to whether the cyclical movements, after they are once started, are self-generating, or whether the movements are either continuously or at intervals reënforced by fresh disturbing forces.

This question is not precisely the same as the question whether the modern economic order is characteristically one of stable or unstable equilibrium. Even though it is admitted that instability is a normal characteristic, so to speak, in the modern order, the question still remains whether this instability is self-generating or whether there are operating upon it external forces which set these wavelike movements going.

In the first place, it is to be noted that the self-generating theory, if accepted, leaves unexplained the initial cause or causes which set the oscillations going.

[1] Cf. *The Stabilization of Business*, pp. 24–26.

The writers who adhere to the self-generating theory
see no beginning and no end. With Mitchell a theory of
the business cycle must be a "descriptive analysis of the
cumulative changes by which one set of business conditions transforms itself into another set." [1] The cycle
is due to processes which run regularly within the world
of business itself. Prosperity breeds a crisis; the crisis
breeds depression; depression breeds revival. Thus the
processes are unceasing. It follows that a theory of the
business cycle must necessarily be a "descriptive analysis" of the interrelated phases of the cycle. Since there is
no starting point, it is necessary to break into the circle
at some point, but one point is as good as another.

Aftalion similarly conceives the cycle to be a closed
system. Observation reveals perpetual oscillations
rather than a state of equilibrium. Once the equilibrium
is broken (he does not tell us how or when), the alternating series of prosperity and depression will succeed
each other in an endless succession of action and reaction.[2] Once slight fluctuations in the demand for
consumers' goods are admitted, you have an adequate explanation for the enormous fluctuations in the
capital-producing industries, and these fluctuations
in turn react upon the demand for consumers' goods.
Thus the oscillations once started tend to perpetuate
themselves. It is the interrelations of the demand for
consumers' goods and the demand for fixed capital

[1] *Business Cycles*, p. 449.

[2] *Revue d'économie politique* (1909), pp. 202–203.

which, in a society carrying on production by the capitalistic, or roundabout, process, account for the self-perpetuation of cyclical fluctuations.

Hawtrey agrees that the cycle is self-generating, but for a different reason. There is an inherent tendency toward fluctuations in the modern money economy, with its existing banking institutions and practices. The periodicity of expansion and contraction is the natural result of the slow response of peoples' cash balances to credit movements. Once the cycle is started, the interrelations of reserves, discount rates, bank loans, and cash balances are such that a succession of oscillations is kept going.[1] Were it not for the lag of cash balances, and the consequent alternating excess and deficiency of bank reserves, a stable equilibrium might be reached. It is the lag of cash balances which automatically swings the pendulum and keeps the industrial mechanism constantly oscillating up and down.[2]

Two objections may be raised to the self-generating theories: First, were there no new disturbing factors business men would gradually learn to adjust themselves to the situation in such a manner that, bit by bit, the oscillations would tone down. Take Aftalion's set of interrelated factors. The oscillations grow out of the fact that the capitalistic system of production cannot

[1] For an analysis similar in many respects to Hawtrey's see Alvin H. Hansen, *Cycles of Prosperity and Depression*, pp. 104–110.

[2] Hawtrey, *Good and Bad Trade*, pp. 267–272; *Currency and Credit*, pp. 125–126.

respond instantly to the consumers' demand, since additional capital equipment must first be built to supply the
new demand. Were it not for the fact that it takes *time*
to get the capitalistic system of production going, supply
would always equal demand, and there would be perfect
equilibrium. In terms of Aftalion's analogy, were it not
for the fact that it requires a certain length of time for
the furnace to generate the required heat, the temperature could instantly be adjusted to the demands of the
occupants. But people soon discover the fact of this
time lag and adjust their actions accordingly. The more
perfect the adjustment, the less become the oscillations
of temperature. In like manner, suppose retailers,
wholesalers, and manufacturers learn the dangers of
stocking up with large inventories and follow a hand-
to-mouth buying policy. Suppose, moreover, they discover that because of the time lag current demand for
consumers' goods is not a safe indication of the future
market for consumers' goods, and so develop for the
building of fixed plant a program budgeted over a long
period of time. Would not such policies, by stabilizing
production, in turn steady consumers' demand, and so
progressively reduce the fluctuations until the oscillations completely ceased and economic equilibrium were
reached? The answer is Yes, provided the required conditions of *adequate foresight* and *systematic unified control*
are present. But both these are lacking in the modern
order, which carries on production by means of intensive division of labor. Errors of judgment are bound to

be made, because it is impossible to forecast the future accurately in a highly developed exchange economy using the capitalistic method of production. Imperfect adjustment to the time lag which follows from the use of fixed capital tends to perpetuate the oscillations. Or consider Hawtrey's set of interrelated factors. If bankers have long observed the lag of people's cash balances, may they not learn to anticipate the overexpansion before the belated drain of cash from the banks severely reduces the bank reserves? Again it must be answered that under competitive decentralized banking systems the bankers are helpless even though their foresight were adequate to cope with the situation. Under an unregulated laissez-faire system of banking, stabilization appears to be not only difficult but, indeed, impossible. In an individualistic, competitive economy there is good ground for believing, with Aftalion and Hawtrey, that society cannot adjust itself to the time lags inherent in our capitalistic and money economy, and so the oscillations, once started, tend to perpetuate themselves.

The second objection is more serious. The self-generating theories are guilty of circular reasoning. Each stage of the cycle is explained by the preceding stage, but there is no escape from the circle. Löwe[1] refers to Aftalion's doctrine as an effort to explain the cycle by means of a logical sleight of hand. The point of departure for his theory, the undercapitalization during

[1] Op. cit. pp. 177–178.

depression, is itself in need of explanation. "In reality there is as a matter of fact in the doctrine of Aftalion nothing proved but only described. ... All these ostensible theories are 'descriptive analysis' as Mitchell rightly says of his own." [1]

Spiethoff, on the other hand, as Löwe points out, gets out of the circle by pointing to external factors such as the discovery of new resources, new inventions, and the like as causative forces starting the up-swing movement.[2] The same may be said of Moore's rainfall-cycle theory. Other writers who give weight to these external factors, as we have seen, are Fisher, Schumpeter, Robertson, Pigou, Cassel, and Adams.

[1] Löwe, op. cit. p. 178. Aftalion's theory in a nutshell contends (1) that slight fluctuations in consumer demand produce wide fluctuations in the production of fixed capital, and (2) that these fluctuations in consumer demand are generated out of prior conditions which have developed from preceding stages in the cycle. We have, however, noted before that it is quite possible to hold (contrary to Aftalion's main thesis) that fluctuations in consumer demand either wholly or in part serve as independent forces from which fluctuations in the demand for fixed capital are derived without admitting that these fluctuations in consumer demand arise out of prior conditions developed within the cycle itself. Fluctuation in consumer demand may spring from outside forces independent of the cycle mechanism, such as the inventions of new products with the consequent *shifts* in consumer demand, large crops, etc. It should be noted, however, that Aftalion himself did give a measure of qualified support to such independent variables as new wants and technical discoveries (cf. *Revue d'économie politique*, 1909, pp. 216–218). Similarly, Mitchell, at points, concedes the impact of independent forces such as wars, crops, etc.; but he holds that on the whole they modify the course of the cycle and are not significant as initiators of the cycle (cf. *Business Cycles*, pp. 452, 473, 512).

[2] See also Joseph Schumpeter, *Theorie der wirtschaftlichen Entwicklung*, p. 352. Duncker & Humblot, 1926.

Hawtrey's analysis is not wholly circular. In so far as the disparity between the loan-market rate of interest and the productivity rate is a result of conditions developing out of previous stages of the cycle, the reasoning is circular; but in so far as this disparity is caused by independent factors such as the discovery of new resources, new markets, new inventions, etc., the reasoning is not circular. Hawtrey lays far greater stress on the former, it is true, but he does not wholly overlook the latter.[1] Fisher, who also uses the Marshall-Wicksell interest-rate analysis, has the merit of definitely escaping the circular reasoning and of finding the explanation of the disparity between the loan rate and the productivity rate in such external factors as inventions, new markets, and large crops.

Most of the writers who escape the circular reasoning admit that once the cycle is started it tends, for a considerable time at least, to be self-generating.[2] Fisher holds that the oscillations gradually weaken just as the arc through which a pendulum swings gradually becomes shorter unless an external force is continually applied. If we pull a twig and let it snap back, we set up a swaying movement back and forth; but the twig, once deflected and then left to itself, soon stops swaying. Friction brings it to rest. So in business: we must

[1] Cf. R. G. Hawtrey, *Good and Bad Trade*, p. 76. Constable and Company, Limited.

[2] Adams, however, holds that each cycle tends to terminate in equilibrium. Cf. A. B. Adams, *Economics of Business Cycles*. McGraw-Hill Company.

assume that the effect of any initial disturbance would soon wear off after a very few oscillations of rapidly diminishing amplitude. The business cycle would soon cease altogether if dependent only on its own reactions. To keep it up, there must be applied some outside force.[1]

Cassel similarly holds that there is a tendency toward a gradual toning down of the upward and downward movements as a result of restrictive reactions. For a limited time the principle of action and reaction produces a set of recurring waves. The restrictive forces operating through the price-building process would gradually bring about a balancing of the upward and downward movements did not fresh disturbing forces independent of the cycle movements develop from the outside.[2]

If this view is correct, if the violence of the cycle and even the continuance of the cycle is dependent upon fresh disturbing factors such as technical inventions, new resources, new markets, new products, new habits of consumers, crop fluctuations, wars, etc., what of the future of business cycles? Is it safe to conclude that the leading disturbing factors are weakening?

So far as the discovery of new resources are concerned, it seems doubtful that the world will ever again witness so significant an event as the exploitation of the resources of America. Never again will the human race have another opportunity to exploit such a large rich

[1] Irving Fisher, "Our Unstable Dollar and the So-called Business Cycle," *Journal of American Statistical Association*, June, 1925.

[2] Gustav Cassel, *The Theory of Social Economy*, pp. 618–623. Harcourt, Brace and Company.

continent. In this respect the nineteenth century bids fair to become unique. The discovery and exploitation of America's rich resources were dynamic factors of the first magnitude. In comparison the backward countries that remain to be developed can be absorbed into the industrial system with less shock and dislocation.

In the second place, while the era of inventions and technical innovations is far from over, yet with the elaborate and complicated modern technical plant already established, no future inventions are likely to have such large disturbing effects as the railroads, for example. It is one thing to have the old technique swept away completely by the steam engine and the railroad; it is quite a different thing for the highly developed machine industry to absorb piecemeal new inventions and improvements. During the nineteenth century Europe and America suffered the birth pangs of a violent transition from a rural order to an industrialized economy.

In the third place, we are reaching a period in which the influence of weather conditions and crop fluctuations have less disturbing effects. And this for three reasons: first, because the whole world is now tied together with a network of swift communications, so that failures in one region are balanced by good harvests in another; secondly, because agriculture has become more diversified; thirdly, because agriculture plays a much smaller rôle relatively in the modern order.

In the fourth place, although wars still remain to cause profound dislocations of industry, possibly when the whole world is brought into the industrial system, when economic imperialism has run its course, this disturbing factor will be minimized.

Finally, business men are gradually accumulating experiences which help them to meet and evade the disturbing factors inherent in the modern system of production. The organization of industry, says Spiethoff, will more and more fit itself to the requirements of the capitalistic manner of industry. The modern means of gaining information, the growing publicity with respect to new opportunities, make for better insight into and control over economic conditions and create a "powerful corrective when men dare too much and lose themselves in excesses."[1] Social control, trade associations, and Kartells, and the control exercised by centralized banking systems are illustrations of an increasing social adjustment to the capitalistic method of production and the money economy. Laissez-faire is gradually being displaced more and more by purposeful and scientific control, not only with respect to discount policies[2] but also with respect to trade competition and intertrade relations. Voluntary associations, even more than governmental regulations, are working in the direction of greater business stability.

[1] Spiethoff, "Vorbemerkungen zu einer Theorie der Überproduction," *Jahrbuch für Gesetzgebung*, 1902, pp. 756–758.

[2] The practical problems with respect to discount policies fall outside the scope of this monograph. Among the writers who have cultivated this intensely interesting field are Wicksell, Cassel, Hahn, Schumpeter, Keynes, Robertson, Pigou, Bellerby, Gregory, Hawtrey, Withers, Lavington, Fisher, Mitchell, Bullock, Sprague, Donham, Commons, Snyder, Beckhart, and B. M. Anderson.

In the last century and a half the capitalistic manner of production has suffered from many "children's diseases," to use Spiethoff's phrase. The exploitation of vast new resources, revolutionary inventions and technics, crop fluctuations in a world still largely dependent upon agriculture, wars, and an uncontrolled credit economy — these are the major disturbing influences that have produced, in the last century and a half, feverish booms and depressions.[1] These dynamic factors are being mitigated, and so the character of the business cycle is changing. The violence of the oscillations of the business cycle during the last hundred and fifty years is the result of a rapidly growing capitalism. In the end it may well be that the cycle phenomenon itself, at least in its extreme manifestations, will be seen to have been a disease which came and passed in the few swift centuries during which the world was made over from a rural, local economy to a highly industrialized world economy. Yet the difficulties of a stable equilibrium in such a complicated order are so great that one must remain skeptical with respect to the feasibility of a genuinely stabilized economic order.

[1] For a stirring discussion of the business cycle as a factor of social change, see Spiethoff, "Krisen," *Handwörterbuch der Staatswissenschaften* (1925), VI, pp. 83–86. The boom of prosperity, with its "sugar-bread of profit," stimulates bold experimentation and daring industrial adventure. On the other side, depression brushes aside inefficient entrepreneurs, and with the "scourge of want" eliminates waste and brings cost-reducing improvements. With respect to social classes and social movements, these upheavals intensify industrial strife, but they make, at the same time, for greater mobility between the various economic classes.

REFERENCES CITED IN FOOTNOTES

ADAMS, A. B. *Economics of Business Cycles.* 1925.

AFTALION, A. "La Réalité des surproductions générales," *Revue d'économie politique*, 1909.

AFTALION, A. *Les Crises périodiques de surproduction*, 1913.

AFTALION, A. "Les Expériences monétaires récentes et la théorie du revenu," *Revue d'économie politique*, May–June, 1925.

AFTALION, A. "La Théorie psychologique de la monnaie," *Revue d'économie politique*, July–August, 1925.

ANDERSON, B. M. "Bank Money and the Capital Supply," *The Chase Economic Bulletin*, November 8, 1926.

ANGELL, J. W. *The Theory of International Prices.* 1926.

BELLERBY, J. R. *The Control of Credit.* 1923.

BELLERBY, J. R. *Monetary Stability.* 1925.

BERGLUND, A. "The United States Steel Corporation and Price Stabilization," *Quarterly Journal of Economics*, November, 1923.

BERGLUND, A. "The United States Steel Corporation and Industrial Stabilization," *Quarterly Journal of Economics*, August, 1924.

BERRIDGE, W. A. *Purchasing Power of the Consumer.* 1925.

BEVERIDGE, W. H. *Unemployment.* 1909.

BICKERDIKE, C. F. "A Non-Monetary Cause of Fluctuations in Employment," *Economic Journal*, September, 1914.

BICKERDIKE, C. F. "Individual and Social Interests in Relation to Saving," *Economic Journal*, September, 1924.

BICKERDIKE, C. F. "Saving and the Monetary System," *Economic Journal*, September, 1925.

BÖHM-BAWERK, E. V. *The Positive Theory of Capital.* 1891.

BOUNIATIAN, M. "Ma Théorie des crises et les critiques de M. Aftalion," *Revue d'économie politique*, 1924.

207

BURTON, T. E. *Financial Crises.* 1902.

CARVER, T. N. "A Suggestion for a Theory of Industrial Depressions," *Quarterly Journal of Economics,* May, 1903.

CASSEL, GUSTAV. *The Theory of Social Economy.* 1924.

CLARK, J. M. "Business Acceleration and the Law of Demand," *Journal of Political Economy,* 1917.

CLARK, J. M. "Some Social Aspects of Overhead Costs," *American Economic Review,* Supplement, 1923.

CLARK, J. M. *The Economics of Overhead Costs.* 1924.

COMMONS, J. R. (with H. L. MCCRACKEN and W. E. ZEUCH). "Secular Trends and Business Cycles," *Review of Economic Statistics.* 1922.

EDIE, L. D. (Editor). *The Stabilization of Business.* 1923.

ENGLAND, M. T. "Analysis of the Crises Cycle," *Journal of Political Economy,* October, 1913.

ENGLAND, M. T. "Promotion as the Cause of Crises," *Quarterly Journal of Economics,* August, 1915.

FISHER, IRVING. *The Rate of Interest.* 1907.

FISHER, IRVING. *Purchasing Power of Money.* 1913.

FISHER, IRVING. "Our Unstable Dollar and the So-called Business Cycle," *Journal of American Statistical Association,* June, 1925.

FOSTER, WILLIAM T., and CATCHINGS, WADDILL. *Money.* 1923.

FOSTER, WILLIAM T., and CATCHINGS, WADDILL. *Profits.* 1925.

FRANK, L. K. "A Theory of Business Cycles," *Quarterly Journal of Economics,* August, 1923.

GIDE, CHARLES, and RIST, CHARLES. *History of Economic Doctrines.*

GIFFEN, ROBERT. *Essays in Finance.* 1896.

GREGORY, T. E. "What can Central Banks Really Do," *American Economic Review,* March, 1925.

GUNTON, GEORGE. *Wealth and Progress.* 1887.

HAHN, ALBERT. *Geld und Kredit.* 1924.

HAHN, ALBERT. "Zur Frage des volkswirtschaftlichen Erkenntnisinhalts der Bankbilanzziffern," *Vierteljahrshefte zur Konjunkturforschung,* 1. Jahrgang, 1926, Ergänzungsheft 4.

HALM, GEORG. "Das Zinsproblem am Geld- und Kapitalmarkt," *Jahrbücher für Nationalökonomie und Statistik*, July and August, 1926.

HANSEN, A. H. *Cycles of Prosperity and Depression.* 1921.

HANSEN, A. H. "Prime Costs in the Business Cycle," *Journal of Political Economy*, February, 1924.

HANSEN, A. H. "Factors affecting the Trend of Real Wages," *American Economic Review*, March, 1925.

HARDY, C. O. *Risk and Risk-Bearing.* 1923.

HASTINGS, H. B. *Costs and Profits.* 1923.

HAWTREY, R. G. *Good and Bad Trade.* 1913.

HAWTREY, R. G. *Currency and Credit.* 1919.

HAWTREY, R. G. *Monetary Reconstruction.* 1923.

HAWTREY, R. G. "Mr. Robertson on Banking Policy," *Economic Journal*, September, 1926.

HEXTER, M. B. *Social Consequences of Business Cycles.* 1925.

HOBSON, J. A. *The Industrial System.* 1909.

HOBSON, J. A. *Economics of Unemployment.* 1922.

HULL, G. H. *Industrial Depressions.* 1911.

JEROME, HARRY. *Migration and Business Cycles.* 1927.

JOHANNSEN, N. *Neglected Point in Connection with Crises.* 1908.

JOHANNSEN, N. *Business Depressions, their Cause* (pamphlet), December, 1925.

KEYNES, J. M. *Monetary Reform.* 1923.

KING, W. I. "Business Cycles, their Cause," *American Contractor*, March 3, 1923.

KNIGHT, F. H. *Risk, Uncertainty, and Profit.* 1921.

KOVALSKAYA, L. M. "The Purchasing Power of Cereals in Connection with the General Fluctuations of Economic Conditions," *The Problems of Economic Conditions*, Vol. III, Issue I. The Conjuncture Institute, Moscow, 1927.

KUZNETS, SIMON S. *Cyclical Fluctuations*, 1926.

LAUDERDALE, J. M. *An Inquiry into the Nature and Origin of Public Wealth.* 1804; 2d ed., 1819.

LAVINGTON, F. *The Trade Cycle.* 1922.

LAYTON, W. T. *Is Unemployment Inevitable?* 1924.

LEDERER, EMIL. "Konjunktur und Krisen,"*Grundriss der Sozial-ökonomik,* 1925.

LESCURE, JEAN. *Des Crises générales et périodiques de surproduction.* 1907; 2d ed., 1923.

LIEFMANN, ROBERT. *Allgemeine Volkswirtschaftslehre.* 1924.

LLOYD, E. M. H. *Stabilization.* 1923.

LÖWE, ADOLPH. "Wie ist Konjunkturtheorie überhaupt möglich?" in *Weltwirtschaftliches Archiv,* October, 1926.

MACGREGOR, D. H. "Sanctions for Discount Policy," *Economic Journal,* December, 1924.

MALTHUS, T. R. *Principles of Political Economy.* 1820.

MANN, L. B. "A National Index of Retail Trade," *Journal of American Statistical Association,* December, 1921.

MARSHALL, ALFRED. *Principles of Economics.* 1890; 7th ed., 1916.

MARSHALL, ALFRED. *Money, Credit, and Commerce.* 1923.

MARSHALL, ALFRED. *Official Papers.* 1926.

MARTIN, P. W. *The Flaw in the Price System.* 1924.

MARX, KARL (with ENGELS, F.). *Communist Manifesto.* 1848.

MARX, KARL. *Das Kapital.* Vol. I, 1867; Vol. II, 1885; Vol. III, 1894 (Kerr edition).

MILL, JAMES. *Elements of Political Economy.* 1821; 3d ed., 1826.

MILL, J. S. *Principles of Political Economy.* 1848; Ashley edition, 1909.

MITCHELL, T. W. "Competitive Illusion as Cause of Business Cycles," *Quarterly Journal of Economics,* August, 1924.

MITCHELL, WESLEY C. *Business Cycles.* 1913.

MITCHELL, WESLEY C. "Controlling Business Cycles," *American Economic Review,* Supplement, 1922.

MITCHELL, WESLEY C. *Business Cycles and Unemployment.* 1923.

MITCHELL, WESLEY C. *Business Annals.* 1926.

MITCHELL, WESLEY C. *Business Cycles: The Problem and its Setting,* 1927.

MITCHELL, W. F. "Interest Cost and the Business Cycle," *American Economic Review,* June, 1926.

MOORE, H. L. *Economic Cycles.* 1914.

MOORE, H. L. *Generating Economic Cycles.* 1923.

MOULTON, H. G. "Commercial Banking and Capital Formation," *Journal of Political Economy*, November, 1918.

OHLIN, BERTIL. "Knut Wicksell," *Economic Journal*, September, 1926.

PERSONS, W. M. "Production, Prices and Aggregate Value of Crops," *Review of Economic Statistics*, 1921.

PIGOU, A. C. *Economics of Welfare.* 1920.

PIGOU, A. C. "Correctives of the Trade Cycle," in *Is Unemployment Inevitable?* 1924.

PIGOU A. C. *Industrial Fluctuations.* 1927.

PUTNAM, G. E. "Paper Profits and Business Cycles," *Harvard Business Review*, 1926.

RICARDO, D. *Principles of Political Economy and Taxation.* 1817; Gonner's edition, 1903.

ROBERTSON, D. H. *A Study of Industrial Fluctuations.* 1915.

ROBERTSON, D. H. *Banking Policy and the Price Level.* 1926.

RÖPKE, WILHELM. "Kredit und Konjunktur," *Jahrbücher für Nationalökonomie und Statistik*, March–April, 1926.

SCHMIDT, F. "Die Industriekonjunktur — ein Rechenfehler! " in *Zeitschrift für Betriebswirtschaft*, 2. Sonderheft, 1927.

SCHUMPETER, J. "Die Wellenbewegung des Wirtschaftslebens," *Archiv für Sozialwissenschaft und Sozialpolitik*, 1914.

SCHUMPETER, J. "Kreditkontrolle," *Archiv für Sozialwissenschaft und Sozialpolitik*, 1925.

SCHUMPETER, J. *Theorie der wirtschaftlichen Entwicklung.* 1926.

SHAPOSHNIKOFF, N. "Credit and Conjuncture," *The Problems of Economic Conditions*, in Vol. III, Issue I. The Conjuncture Institute, Moscow, 1927.

SIDGWICK, HENRY. *Principles of Political Economy.* 1883; 1901.

SNYDER, CARL. "Influence of Interest Rate on the Business Cycle," *American Economic Review*, December, 1925.

SOMBART, W. *Das Wirtschaftsleben im Zeitalter des Hochkapitalismus*, 1927.

212   REFERENCES CITED IN FOOTNOTES

SPIETHOFF, ARTHUR. "Vorbemerkungen zu einer Theorie der Überproduktion," *Jahrbuch für Gesetzgebung, Verwaltung und Volkswirtschaft*, 1902.

SPIETHOFF, ARTHUR. "Die Krisentheorien von M. v. Tougan-Baranowsky und L. Pohle," *Jahrbuch für Gesetzgebung, Verwaltung und Volkswirtschaft*, 1903.

SPIETHOFF, ARTHUR. "Krisen," *Handwörterbuch der Staatswissenschaften*, 1925.

SPRAGUE, O. M. W. "Discount Policy of Federal Reserve Bank," *American Economic Review*, March, 1921.

TAUSSIG, F. W. *Principles of Economics.* 1921.

TAYLOR, F. M. *Principles of Economics.* 1921.

THORNTON, H. *An Enquiry into the Nature and Effects of the Paper Credit of Great Britain.* 1802.

TOUGAN-BARANOWSKY, M. *Les Crises industrielles en Angleterre.* 1913.

VEBLEN, THORSTEIN B. *The Theory of Business Enterprise.* 1904.

VEBLEN, THORSTEIN B. *The Engineers and the Price System.* 1921.

VOGEL, E. H. *Die Theorie des volkswirtschaftlichen Entwickelungsprozesses und das Krisenproblem.* 1917.

WARREN, G. F., and PEARSON, F. A. *The Agricultural Situation,* 1924.

WICKSELL, KNUT. "The Influence of the Rate of Interest on Prices," *Economic Journal*, June, 1907.

YOUNG, ALLYN A. "Hawtrey, Currency and Credit; Fisher, Stabilizing the Dollar," *Quarterly Journal of Economics*, 1920.

YOUNG, ALLYN A. "The Trend of Prices," *American Economic Review*, Supplement, March, 1923.

YOUNG, ALLYN A. "Bank Statistics for the United States," *Review of Economic Statistics*, 1925.

INDEX

218 INDEX